JOY

in Every Moment

Mindful Exercises for Waking to the Wonders of Ordinary Life

Tzivia Gover

Illustrations by O'

Storey Publishing

The mission of Storey Publishing is to serve our customers by
publishing practical information that encourages
personal independence in harmony with the environment.

Edited by Deborah Balmuth and Sarah Guare
Art direction and book design by Jessica Armstrong

Illustrations by © Olaf Hajek

Storey Publishing
210 MASS MoCA Way
North Adams, MA 01247
www.storey.com

Printed in China by R.R. Donnelley
10   9   8   7   6   5   4   3   2   1

Library of Congress Cataloging-in-Publication Data

Gover, Tzivia.
 Joy in every moment : mindful exercises for waking to the wonders of ordinary life
/ Tzivia Gover.
     pages cm
  ISBN 978-1-61212-511-4 (pbk. : alk. paper)
  ISBN 978-1-61212-512-1 (ebook) 1. Meditation. 2. Joy. I. Title.
BL624.2.G678 2015
158.1'2—dc23
                           2015027646

For Miranda,
who came into this world
with her light shining bright,
and who teaches
and inspires me — even when
she doesn't know it.

ACKNOWLEDGMENTS

I have been lavishly blessed with a close, caring family and deep and loving friendships, as well as with teachers (those who knowingly signed up for the job and many more who didn't). I am constantly aware of — and awake to — the fact that this book, as well as the richness and beauty of my life, are the result of the amazing people I am so lucky to know and who support me with their wisdom and love. Here are just a few who have in some way touched and blessed this project:

Deborah Balmuth and Sarah Guare, along with all the creative, dedicated folks at Storey Publishing; Mitchell S. Waters of the Curtis Brown Literary Agency; my family of dreamers at the International Association for the Study of Dreams; Aja Riggs, Anita Gallers, Betsy Grund, Claudia V. Johnsen, Diane Gover, Dick Gover, Elise Gibson, Gale Fralin, Grace Welker, Hermine Mensink, James Gover, Jane Covell, Joanne Yoshida, Justina Lasley, Karen Levy, Laura Baughman, Lesléa Newman, Lori Soderlind, Louis Moore, Miranda Sanders, Molly Hale, Rachel Hass, Rachel Kuhn, Riva Danzig, Sherry Treadaway-Puricelli, Sylvia Green-Guenette, and Virginia Pasternak; Patricia Lee Lewis and everyone at the Patchwork Farms Writers Retreat in Culebra; and Susan Stinson and the Writers Room at Forbes Library.

Thank you all for filling my life with joy!

Contents

Keep a green tree
in your heart
and perhaps
a singing bird
will come.

Chinese Proverb

Hunting Down
HAPPY MEMORIES

On hearing a friend talk about her happy memories of childhood once, I complained that I didn't have joyful memories from being small. I was in my thirties, and I believed I'd had a terrible childhood. I had plenty of evidence to back up my claim: my parents divorced when I was entering my teen years, my father had an explosive temper, and my siblings and I fought incessantly. Not only did I have very few happy memories, at the time I had very few childhood memories, period.

But my friend wasn't buying my bleak assessment of my past. "You must have had some happy moments growing up," she insisted.

Determined to prove her wrong, I lay in bed that night trying to conjure up a happy memory from my grammar school days or earlier. I searched my past for anything: a color, a sound, a flash of memory that I could tug on, and that might unfurl a scene of pleasure; a little something that would make me smile to remember.

At first I just found myself staring into a vast, textured darkness. I thought the darkness confirmed my belief that there were no happy scenes to illuminate it, but perhaps it was simply the darkness of eyes squeezed shut, blocking out the parts of the picture that didn't fit the story I'd been telling myself for so long.

As I continued to squint into the past, I remembered something I'd learned on a guided hike through the woods in New England. The secret to tracking animals, the leader explained, is to place in your mind's eye a "search image" of the paw print, or of the bird or animal you're looking for. You practice seeing it in your mind so you will recognize what you are looking for when you find it.

If I were to develop a search image for happiness, I wondered, what would it look like? Would it be brightly colored? Would it be a fluffy pink or sunny orange?

With these questions in mind, I sifted through memories of rooms and landscapes, until I saw the backyard at my grand-parents' house, decades ago when I was about 4 years old and my grandmother was still alive. I saw myself on the spring-green grass that edges up to the still blue water at the edge of their property. I remembered being happy playing there, under the arcing branches of the willow tree. I fell asleep with my sweet memory tucked beside me like a child's stuffed animal, my arm thoughtlessly brushing against it all night while I slept.

For the nights and weeks that followed, I repeated this exercise. Little by little I began to amass a collection of happy memories. I kept a notebook by my bed in which to record them, until eventually I no longer had to hunt so hard to capture and collect them.

For some people happiness comes easily. For more of us, we need to be active participants in the quest to attain it. As it turns out, both stories I tell myself are true. There were indeed very difficult parts of my childhood. But there was love, laughter, and joy, too. Seeing the whole picture, not just selected scenes, helps me to be fully who I am.

Healing is the process of becoming whole, and when I reflect on what I am most proud of in my life, it is the healing work I have done. That work has included forgiving, learning to choose love over fear at every turn, and affirming my commitment to self-growth and happiness by looking for the best in myself, in others, and in every situation I encounter.

I wrote this book to affirm my own process, and to offer it to you as something of a field guide to keep with you as you continue on your journey to a more joyful life.

EXERCISES *for the Joy of It*

Battle Scars

Write the story of a scar you have, or of your wrinkles, or stretch marks. Describe this seeming imperfection in detail, and write out how you got it and the lessons it has taught you.

Click and Keep

If you have a camera on your phone, snap pictures of small details from your day that you can tuck away as happy memories: the vibrant blue of a dropped glove on a sidewalk, rays of golden sunset behind a mountain of clouds, a rainbow swirl of graffiti on a crumbling building, or the first crocus at the edge of a tide of melting snow.

Stalking Joy

Whether you have few happy memories or photo albums stuffed with them, call the good times to mind as you lie in bed ready to fall asleep, when you're waiting for a bus or a subway train, or while you're on hold waiting for a customer service rep to come onto the phone line.

Harvest Happiness

Collect images, colors, words, and phrases from magazines that remind you of happy moments and good feelings. Create collages of these impressions and post them around your house in prominent places (the refrigerator door, your bathroom mirror) or protected ones (on the inside of your closet door so you can sneak a peek each morning as you choose your clothes for the day, on the inside cover of your journal, etc.).

Begin Again

Happy Baby Pose is a yoga posture that calms our thoughts and reduces stress and fatigue. Lie on your back with bent knees and point the soles of your feet toward the ceiling, letting your thighs splay comfortably at 45-degree angles to the floor. Hold your big toes with your thumb and first finger, or hold onto the outsides of your feet. If it's comfortable, rock gently back and forth. Maintain the pose for 30 seconds or a minute. You might just hear the tinkling bells of childhood joy ringing.

We're all happy,
if we only knew it.

Woody Allen, *Shadows and Fog*

JOY: *The User's Manual*

Perhaps you've read about the studies showing that people who feel grateful, think positively, and connect meaningfully with others are happier. You want to be happier, too, so you've tried keeping gratitude lists, and you try to remember to remind yourself to look on the bright side — but after a day or two, well, you forget. As for joining a support group or volunteering to create more meaningful connections in your life — sounds great, but who's got the time?

That's the problem. As simple as it sounds to put a smile on your face and be happy, habits of negative thinking, complaining, and rushing through what might otherwise have been rich moments are not so easy to break. But here's the good news: like the sun in the sky even on a cloudy day, joy is always shining inside you. All you really need to do is make subtle adjustments to create clarity and feel its sustaining warmth and beauty.

Joy in Every Moment offers simple, fun — and sometimes surprising — tips and techniques you can try on your own or with others to bring more of this delightful expansiveness into your days. Page by page, I invite you to wake into the present moment where you can discover the gifts your life is already offering you — even when you're too busy or distracted to notice.

How to Use This Book

A Page a Day

Just as this book encourages you to savor each moment, so too will you benefit from leafing slowly and intentionally through its pages. On each one you will find something to help you shift your perspective, reawaken your senses, and celebrate your life as it unfolds, day by day and moment by moment.

Joy Journal

Purchase a notebook or journal to use for the various exercises in this book, and also use it to note your evolving thoughts on what constitutes a life of meaning and joy for you.

Between the Covers

You may want to read this book straight through, or you may want to dip in and out of different sections depending on what topics are calling to you most strongly. Feel free to flip through the pages to get familiar with what is offered here, then read the sections in whatever order feels right to you.

Join with Others

Invite a friend or family member to commit to practicing joy with you. Read this book together, and check in weekly to share successes, set intentions, and get support to help you stay on track.

Keep Joy Close at Hand

Carry this book in your pocket or purse, or leave it on a bedside table or kitchen counter to invite quick access. Reach for it whenever you need a gentle reminder to enjoy!

Practical Application

Reading this book promises to be enjoyable on its own, but the real rewards come from putting the tips and techniques into practice. Choose at least one suggestion a day from these pages and try it. Remember, the joy is in the doing.

one

Introducing Joy

Happiness is
two kinds of ice cream.
Knowing a secret.
Climbing a tree.

Happiness is
five different crayons.
Catching a firefly.
Setting him free.

Clark Gesner,
You're a Good Man, Charlie Brown

You Are JOY

I can't remember what prompted me to ask the question, but I'll never forget the answer. Several years back, I asked my mother, "What was I like as a small child?"

She could have answered in any number of ways. For example, I remember my siblings called me a crybaby. My father, with a mix of love and impatience in his voice, used to call me a pest. I once overheard a family friend describe me as a nervous kid. I remember being bossy, moody, friendly, and studious.

So my mother's answer took me by surprise. Without hesitation she replied, "You were a joy."

A joy? This was not even in the ballpark of what I'd been anticipating. I'd done years of therapy, read dozens of self-help books, and participated in numerous self-growth classes, all of which I believed had made me into a happier person, the underlying assumption being I'd been a bit gloomy before.

But after my mother's pronouncement, that at age 4, or 5, or 6, I was already "a joy," I had an epiphany. Despite all my earnest striving toward becoming a better person, I now realized that I didn't need to work so hard. What I really had to do instead was, well, be myself; be my *true* self, that is. Underneath all of my labels, stories, selective memories, and assumptions about how others saw me, I already was the person I'd been trying so diligently to become. I was joy.

This is an example of waking up to truth. Instead of signing up for one more workshop, buying one more transformational CD or how-to book, I simply had to embrace my joyful nature.

It is easy to imagine my own daughter, grown now, asking me the same question someday. And if she does, I won't hesitate. I remember the first moment I laid eyes on her. I saw in her newborn self a light glowing as if from within. I saw her radiant joy as plainly as I saw her little potato-shaped nose and pink newborn body.

But with all she has gone through in the intervening years — the struggles, disappointments, and challenges, along with the triumphs and shining moments — I imagine she'd be as surprised by my answer as I was by my mother's.

So many of us believe that to be joyous we need to do a lot of work. But the truth is, our essence is already sparkling with happiness and bliss. All we really need to do is cultivate good internal habits to allow our divine spark to be revealed.

My mother knew this about me all along, and I know it about my daughter.

It is true of you, too.

EXERCISES *for the Joy of It*

Affirm Joy

Wake to the idea that you *are* joy. Use this phrase today as an affirmation: "I am joy." Each time you repeat the words inwardly to yourself, feel a spark deep inside you growing into a bright star, then a bold sun.

Up in the Sky

Step outside or look out the window. No matter what the weather — clouds, snow, rain, storm, fog, or clear — remind yourself that the sun and stars are always shining, whether you can see them in that moment or not.

Baby Steps

Watch children playing, and notice how quickly they find a reason to dance, wonder, or laugh. Tear storms come and go; smiles are never far behind. Now it's your turn. Give yourself permission to feel your feelings without judging them or assigning too much weight to them. Can you have a good cry, then turn up the music and dance in the living room?

Find a place inside
where there's joy,
and the joy
will burn out the pain.

Joseph Campbell

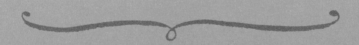

How Do YOU *Spell Joy?*

Joy. It's a small, simple word composed of three letters: a curvy *J,* a perfect *O,* and an exuberant, sky-hugging *Y.* It's a word that might wear pink or purple and possess a fondness for exclamation points. Peppy and compact, it is often misunderstood. It's a word that's been worn down from overuse, appropriated by advertising campaigns, and relegated to coy catch phrases splashed across greeting cards and souvenir T-shirts.

Poor, misunderstood Joy; it can seem as though its very popularity and desirability have conspired to make some suspicious of its true meaning. Joy is like a girl who just happens to be good at cheerleading, who can jump up and effortlessly make her spine into an elastic arc — who really does wake up happy in the morning — but who is mistaken for trite, clichéd, or shallow.

Joy, however, is anything but saccharine or false. It is delight; a fully embodied form of contentment. It's the smile that finds its own stretch and doesn't need to be tugged into place. It's what the morning glory does when it feels the first rays of sunlight on its petals. It's the splash that sends a feeding fish slaphappy out of the water, and it's the flick of its tail on its return. Joy is the impulse in the morning that sends you into the kitchen for tea and toast before the alarm has had a chance to ring. It's the feeling palm leaves must have when they riffle the air in the Caribbean breeze. And it might just make you feel like you want to give a little jump for . . . well, yes . . . joy!

EXERCISES *for the Joy of It*

Defining Terms

The dictionary describes joy as a feeling of great pleasure and happiness. But the best definition for joy comes from within you. Take 5 to 10 minutes and write your own definition. What does joy mean to you?

Shades of Joy

Good feelings come in all varieties. Make a list of all the different gradations of happiness you experience, from glad to giddy, easygoing to ecstatic. See how your mood is elevated simply by thinking about positive emotions.

Mine the Moments

Make a list of moments when you've felt joy. Choose one or two instances and describe them in detail. What were you doing? Who were you with? Where were you? Did joy take you by surprise? What were the events that led up to the feeling?

When the mind is pure,
joy follows like a shadow
that never leaves.

Buddha

5 RULES *on the Road to Happiness*

Sometimes joy seems mysterious. We meet someone who has suffered great losses, yet she seems to glow with gratitude and ease. And then we spend time with an uncle who is blessed with wealth and health but who can do nothing but scowl, growl, and complain. Science tells us that to some extent, our level of happiness is set by our genetic makeup and our life circumstances. But research shows, and evidence abounds, that we each have the capacity to increase our level of happiness. Sure, having some money in the bank helps, but being happy has more to do with the cultivation of habits of attitude and building the muscles of resiliency, rather than with our outer circumstances. It's the practice of such intangible traits as generosity, optimism, and compassion that puts a spring in the step of those who seem to be having a slightly better time at the party — even when there isn't one.

There are no rules for how to be happy. But there are some basic principles that faith traditions from across cultures and through the ages agree on, and that science supports. Here are some guidelines to help you shift into a brighter mood.

1. **IT'S YOUR MOOD.** We may feel that we are at the whim of our moods and emotions, but we have a lot more control over how we feel than we think. Anyone can increase his level of joy and

happiness by choosing where to put his attention (on negative or positive thoughts, on people who uplift him or those who drain energy from him) and creating and maintaining positive intentions.

2. **IT'S AN INSIDE JOB.** No one else can make you happy. That's the good news — and the not-so-good news. It's good news because others don't have control of how you experience your life. The not-so-good news, perhaps, is that you need to take the initiative to consciously choose which thoughts and attitudes to focus on, and to choose healthy reactions to the people and events in your life.

3. **YOU CAN HAVE IT NOW.** You don't have to wait to get a new job, the perfect partner, or your dream house to feel good. External events, possessions, or situations don't guarantee deep or long-term happiness. But a daily commitment to feeling better can.

4. **THE PURSUIT IS WHAT WE'RE PROMISED.** Our founding fathers were wise in promising us the *pursuit* of happiness. No one can guarantee your good spirits because finding true contentment is an active and ongoing process. Living a full and meaningful life requires a commitment to healthy ways of being.

5. **THERE IS A FAST TRACK TO FEELING GOOD.** Yes, living a joyful life takes some initiative and effort, but it's by no means dreary hard work. In fact, there are shortcuts to feeling better. Shifting your thoughts and feelings to gratitude and loving-kindness are quick ways to connect with your joyous heart.

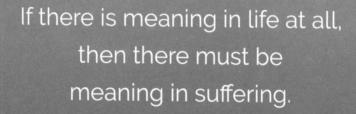

If there is meaning in life at all,
then there must be
meaning in suffering.

Viktor Frankl

The OY *of Joy*

Some days it seems joy is everywhere: It's in the sun hitting the terra-cotta tiles on the side of a building, or in the rush of delight at seeing a rainbow after a storm. You notice that people are smiling at you as you walk down the street between the bank and your car, and you wonder why. Then you notice that you've been smiling at them. Some days it's that easy.

Other days you're caring for a parent who is recovering in the ICU, you're trying to comfort your spouse who is afraid of being the next one to be laid off, or your daughter calls to tell you her marriage is in trouble. On these days, joy seems like a word from a foreign language that you can't translate.

We know about joy because we know sadness. We know the joy of letting go because we know the desperate sorrow of being ripped off, or of being denied the love of someone we yearn for. We find joy in the middle of the night just after crying our last tear, and the tear after that.

This knowledge of the connection between separation and wholeness, heartbreak and healing, is reflected in the creation story from the Kabbalah, the Jewish mystical tradition, in which the world, once whole and perfect, is broken like a crystal bowl that drops and shatters. The shards, scattered throughout the world, must be put back together. This story hints at the beauty of the brokenness we encounter in our lives. It also hints at the splendor of what is possible when we accept the pain of being in pieces, and the power in putting things back together — one tiny piece at a time. While the process might feel lonely at times, the story reminds us that we are neither alone nor powerless as we engage in this effort both individually and with others on our quests for healing.

EXERCISES *for the Joy of It*

Be the Honey

Some days we feel we need to court joy. But sometimes it's better to be the honey, find and flaunt your own sweetness (honesty, clarity, authenticity), and let joy come to you.

Broken Bits of Joy

Mosaics are beautiful pieces of artwork made from shattered bits of glass and broken tile. Today, seek out the beauty in what's broken or abandoned: a dried brown leaf drifting in the wind, bits of shattered green glass along the highway, an abandoned car on a country road with yellow wildflowers pushing up through the hanging fender . . .

Helping Hands

Who are the people you talk to when things are difficult? The ones with whom you can share your secrets and fears? If you don't have relationships that support this type of sharing right now, what steps can you take to deepen an existing friendship to include this type of connection? Individual therapy or support groups can also offer the help that's needed.

Sigh into Sadness

Trying to avoid negative feelings only makes them more powerful. Set a timer for 20 minutes. In that time, allow yourself to feel the contents of your heavy heart. Sigh into the weight of all your sadness, and let go of trying to make it better. Feel the burdens settle down, as if into a hammock that is firmly anchored to two steady trees. Each time you exhale allow yourself to surrender to what is, without attaching judgment or stories to the feelings. Allow the sadness to soften and dissolve. When the timer sounds, exhale with an audible sigh. Get up, and shake out your hands and legs, releasing any stale, stuck energy. Move into your day feeling lighter and brighter.

Let Yourself Cry

When you let the tears flow and quiet the impulse toward blame or regret; when you stay present with your broken heart — it's as if the tears turn to glistening crystals. They may even become surprisingly beautiful drops of joy.

Rock What You've Got

Granted, some people seem to do better in the happiness lottery than others. Genetic factors, economic circumstances, and early childhood experiences are among the factors that account for what some researchers call the happiness set point for each individual. But people can do a lot to increase their levels of happiness regardless of their set point. Accept your current life situation, and commit to taking responsibility for creating more joy in your life from today forward.

Sit with It

Wouldn't it be nice if we could skip past the pain and fast-forward to bliss? The truth is, to experience true contentment, we must be willing to feel all of our emotions, from angst to despair to sadness. And while our natural tendency might be to distract ourselves from discomfort, it is in our willingness to accept what we feel in the moment, acknowledge the emotion, and be willing to let it go that we find true peace.

Meditation is a tool that teaches us to meet ourselves where we are and be with whatever thoughts and feelings arise without attachment or judgment. While the practice of meditation is profound, it is also quite simple to learn. There are many different types of meditation, from walking meditation, to contemplative writing, to meditating on sound or visual objects. But all forms of meditation begin with getting still and quiet inside.

Start slowly: sit in meditation for 5 minutes to start, then try 10, then 15, working up to 20 minutes or more each day. But remember, this is an ongoing practice where perfection has no place. The success lies in the attempt.

Here are some basic instructions to get you started.

1. **CHOOSE A TIME** for your meditation practice. First thing in the morning or in the evening about an hour before bed are two good options. Whatever time you choose, make a commitment to meditating every day by blocking out the time in your planner.

2. **FIND A COMFORTABLE PLACE** to meditate where you won't be disturbed or distracted. Close the door, turn off the phone, and prepare to turn inward.

3. **SIT ON A CUSHION ON THE FLOOR** with legs crossed or in a straight-backed chair with legs uncrossed and feet flat on the floor, or in any way that allows you to sit comfortably with a long spine, so your breath can move freely. It helps to set a timer, so you won't feel the need to check your watch.

4. **GENTLY CLOSE YOUR EYES,** or keep them open and softly focused toward a spot on the floor in front of you.

5. **WITH YOUR MOUTH AND JAW RELAXED** and lips slightly parted, breathe in and out through your nose, noticing the length, quality, and rate of your breath.

Steps continue on page 37

The best way out
is always through.

Robert Frost,
"A Servant to Servants"

6. QUIET YOUR MIND by choosing one or two simple words to focus on. For example, as you inhale silently say "in" and as you exhale silently say "out."

7. IF ANY OTHER THOUGHTS ARISE, return your attention to your breath. It is natural for the mind to wander, so try not to feel frustrated or discouraged.

8. WHEN THE TIMER SOUNDS, open your eyes or lift your gaze and shift your attention back to the world all around you.

9. SMILE, AND CONGRATULATE YOURSELF for taking this time to cultivate a deep and meaningful meditation practice.

10. REPEAT! Your practice will deepen and grow with time. Make a 21-day commitment to daily meditation. When those 21 days are up, recommit to another 21 days, until meditation becomes part of your daily routine.

two

Joy
All Day
Long

Statistically,
the probability of any one
of us being here is so small
that you'd think the mere fact
of existing would keep us all
in a contented dazzlement
of surprise.

Lewis Thomas,
The Lives of a Cell

A DAY *in the* LIFE

What could be more prosaic than an ordinary day? There are 7 in every week, 365 in a year, and the average American will experience nearly 30,000 of them in a lifetime. If familiarity breeds contempt, we live in danger of devaluing the very currency of our lives.

For a mayfly, a day is all there is. Intricately outfitted with seven pairs of gills, two to three long tails, and wings, this tiny creature gets only one day to feed, mate, and experience the lakes and streams where it lives. Some species of moths live for mere minutes. The male ant has a comparatively luxurious several-day life span. From this perspective a day is nothing to squander.

Interestingly, the word *day*, from the Old English *daeg,* shares its etymological roots with the word *lifetime.*

Each day we live a microcosm of our life. Each morning we are born anew, and each night we have the chance to make a full accounting of how we spent our precious hours just before we slip into the mysterious darkness of sleep. We are gifted with tens of thousands of opportunities to master the art of living life fully awake to the wonders of ordinary moments.

EXERCISES *for Joy All Day*

Running Water

Starting with brushing your teeth, each time you turn on a faucet and see water flushing into the sink, consciously exhale all of your tension with a whooshing breath and let your worries cascade down the drain with the water.

Voice Message

When you hear a phone chirp, vibrate, or ring, heed the call by checking in with your internal chatter. Still your inner monologue and listen inside for silence.

One, Two, Three

When you notice your mind wandering to negative or stressful thoughts, close your eyes and take three breaths. With the first breath feel stillness in the center of your body. With the second breath listen to the silence in your mouth and tongue. With the third breath feel within your mind a sense of expansiveness as limitless as a clear blue sky. Smile, open your eyes, and see the world anew.

Thanks Again

When you hear yourself complaining about a person or event in your life, stop and consider three things about that person or situation that you are genuinely grateful for.

Eleven Eleven

Twice a day the readout on your digital clock flashes 11:11. It's just the time of day, but a lot has been made of the 11:11 phenomenon. Some say significant events tend to occur at 11:11, or that it's the perfect time to make a wish. Why not simply use 11:11 as an invitation to wake into the present moment? Each time you notice that it's 11:11, stop and breathe into your heart. Give thanks for all the good things in your day. Keep this mini meditation going — until 11:12, when you resume your activities refreshed and awakened to the day's ordinary wonder.

Take Five

The five senses are like five gateways that help you wake up to the present moment. Notice the colors that surround you; tune in to the sounds; touch something and give it your entire attention for even a moment. Notice the tastes on your tongue. Stop and smell the roses — or any other fragrant flower in your environment.

With EYES WIDE OPEN

Some days you wake happy. On others you wake on the wrong side of the bed, unable all day, it feels like, to see anything positive about your experience. Sometimes it seems you didn't really wake up at all, having run on autopilot from when you brushed your teeth in the morning to when you turned down the bedcovers at night.

Whether you rise to the sounds of trilling birds, or to a beeping, buzzing, or ringing alarm clock, waking up is more than merely getting up and out of bed. From a practical point of view, waking up may be the simple act of opening your eyes in the morning, but from a scientific perspective, waking up is a physiological shift in consciousness, from the brain chemistry of sleep and dreaming to that of wakeful attention.

Mystics and philosophers have long posited that life is a dream and that our job is to wake within it to discover meaning, purpose, beauty, and joy. But too many of us doze through our lives, not fully accessing our potential. We may even unconsciously create conflict and negativity.

Waking up to the present moment inspires and energizes us. Waking up in this way ensures that we won't sleepwalk through life or fall into habitual ways of seeing the world around us.

Truly awakening requires a shift in attitude and perspective. It entails empowering ourselves to experience the gifts and treasures in the life we are already living. Waking up means opening your eyes to the present moment and greeting it with a joyful heart. The simple but profound practices of setting intentions, choosing where to focus your attention, and reflecting on your thoughts and actions are keys to living wide awake.

Throughout the day, try waking up by consciously shifting your awareness from worry to faith, from an attitude of rushing to a mental state of stillness, from anxiety to inner silence, and from fear to love.

Can you open your eyes and your heart to the inherent joy and meaning of your life as you go about the business of caring for your family, your home, your work, and yourself?

The best way to make your dreams come true is to wake up.

Zen Saying

EXERCISES *for Joy All Day*

Get a Move On

Doing even 5 minutes of active exercise in the morning gets your blood flowing and energizes you for the day. Try doing one to three sun salutations, a few stretches, jumping jacks, or taking a brisk walk around the block before breakfast.

Cyclical Thinking

While we sleep, our brain chemistry shifts every 90 minutes between different sleep stages. During daytime hours our brain chemistry also shifts every 90 minutes or so. Honor these cycles by checking in with yourself every 90 minutes throughout the morning — or all day long. Stop to renew and refresh your thoughts with one or more slow, gentle, calming breaths.

Sleep Mode

Our computers and other electronic devices shift into sleep mode many times each day. Whenever you are prompted to "press any key" to wake up your screen, take the opportunity to wake yourself up to the present moment, too.

Don't Hit Snooze

Rather than just roll out of bed in the morning, wake mindfully. Set intentions first thing in the morning and shift from a blah mood to a better day.

Wake Your Heart

When you are waiting for your email messages to load on your smartphone, or for a web page to appear on your laptop screen, take a moment to wake your heart and counteract "screen slump" with a simple exercise. Roll your shoulders back, and feel the tips of your shoulder blades slide down your back toward one another. Then feel your chest open, making more room for your lungs to expand and your heart to blossom like a flower. Now, return to your screen with a more expansive attitude.

Wake to Gratitude

Before your feet touch the floor, feel grateful for the good and safe night's sleep you just experienced. Smile in gratitude for being given another chance to live your best life today.

Wake First

Set a morning phone curfew. Wait until you are fully awake — after you've washed, stretched, and eaten breakfast — before turning on your cell phone.

When you rise
in the morning,
give thanks for the light,
for your life,
for your strength.
Give thanks for your food
and for the joy of living.

Tecumseh

En-Lighten UP

Feeling happy on a sunny day seems easier than on a cold winter afternoon when daylight is scarce. In fact, many people are prone to emotional heaviness brought on by darker days. This makes sense. After all, our bodies are biologically programmed to respond to the sun's rays. Our skin literally drinks in the mood-boosting vitamin D_3 that sunshine provides.

Even our language and the expressions we use reflect this attraction to light. When someone needs cheering we encourage him to "lighten up," and when we want to do good in the world we try to "be a light for others." When someone achieves a state of equanimity and bliss we say she is "enlightened."

There are many ways to consciously bring light into your life — both literally and metaphorically — whether or not the sun is shining.

EXERCISES *for Joy All Day*

Shine Your Light

Smile brightly when you meet another person, letting your eyes sparkle. Feel your inner light shining through as you go about your daily routines.

Let the Sunshine In

Light helps synchronize our circadian rhythms, and insufficient light can exacerbate states of sadness or depression. To increase your exposure to light, especially in the fall and winter months, spend time outdoors taking a walk, doing yard work, or sitting in the sunshine. Indoors, full-spectrum lightbulbs can give you a boost as well; just be sure not to use them in the evening when your body should be settling down and preparing for sleep.

Wake Up Winter

In the dark winter months, use candles, salt lamps, and strings of white lights to brighten your home with a happy glow.

Sparkle from the Inside Out

Close your eyes and imagine a spark of light inside a lantern at the center of your heart. Each time you inhale, see the spark grow into a gentle flame. As you exhale, sense that light brightening until, breath by breath, it fills your body. Keep breathing until you can imagine this brightness shining through your very pores.

If you change the way
you look at things,
the things you look at change.

Wayne Dyer, *The Power of Intention*

ROSE-COLORED *Glasses*

A February morning in New England is a study in monotones. Pull open the curtains just after dawn, and a landscape of snow, bare trees, and gray skies fills the windowpanes. It's difficult to muster enthusiasm on such a morning.

But then the sun creeps over the horizon, spilling a watery, apricot-colored blush over the snow covering your lawn. It's all there is — little more than the memory of color. But contemplating it for just a moment before turning up the thermostat and putting on the water for tea reveals all you need to know. It's as though the world were winking in your direction, and offering a secret smile.

It's easy to be happy on a sunny day when all is going well. But the joy that seeps in unexpectedly, even on a day when a loved one has left, when work is overwhelming, or it's simply been too cold for too long, has its own sweet flavor that can be savored all day long.

These are the rose-colored glasses nature offers us: sometimes subtle — sometimes glorious — shifts in our attention from bleakness to bloom. It might be the flash of a cardinal's red breast on a winter's day, a patch of sky brightening behind the bare tips of branches beneath the clouds, or a blue sky on a February afternoon — each unexpected beauty reveals the possibility of a gentler view.

But you don't have to wait for something to change to activate this spontaneous sense of wonder. You can choose to look through the lens of love and hope any time, in any season.

EXERCISES *for Joy All Day*

Loving Eyes

There's one decision you can make again and again all day long: choose to see the world through the eyes of love rather than through the eyes of fear. Fear comes in many forms, including jealousy, anxiety, distrust, hatred, anger, resistance, and criticism. When you find yourself responding from a place of fear, stop and soften your heart. Then choose to speak, act, or think from love. Simply say to yourself, "I choose love."

Blink!

Close your eyes and open them again. This time notice the gifts and gold of the present moment.

Mirror, Mirror

Each time you look in the mirror, think of something you appreciate about yourself: your hair, your eyes, the little wrinkles at the corners of your mouth, the kindness you showed to a stranger the other day, or your loving or courageous heart. Focus on this aspect of yourself, and smile into your own eyes looking back at you.

I can scarcely wait
till tomorrow
when a new life
begins for me,
as it does each day,
as it does each day.

Stanley Kunitz,
"The Round"

Good NIGHT

As a child, going to sleep was easy. As bedtime approached you were told to put on your pajamas and wash up. This command elicited a few reluctant pleas for "5 more minutes" of TV or a little more time to finish your game of Monopoly — but no outright rebellion. You sat with your parents on the edge of your bed, and perhaps you said your prayers or you listened to your favorite nursery rhymes read aloud. Then it was time to be tucked in, turn off the lights, and drift into the Land of Nod.

As an adult, with no one issuing the bedtime command, with pajamas seeming like a quaint relic of the past replaced by oversized T-shirts or mismatched thermal underwear sets, and with email and social media sites singing their siren songs, getting into bed has, for many, become more rout than ritual.

The consequences of shortchanging ourselves when it comes to sleep are more serious than receiving a childhood reprimand. Sneaking by on too little sleep affects physical and mental health.

Creating a soothing nighttime routine — at any age — can make all the difference. Send yourself off to sleep consciously by powering down your electronic devices, reading a soothing story before getting into bed, listening to relaxation CDs, or by giving yourself a foot massage with lavender-scented cream. Then you can snuggle into a night of luxurious sleep and dreaming.

EXERCISES *for Joy All Day*

Refreshing Routines

As you prepare for bed, consciously let go of the day as you change into your pajamas, rinse away worries as you wash your face, and wrap yourself in gratitude as you snuggle under the covers. Imbuing bedtime routines with intention can help you enter sleep more consciously, get a better night's sleep, and wake refreshed.

R&R

Take a good look at your bedroom and notice any objects or items that are antithetical to a good night's sleep. Remove distracting elements such as televisions or computers, as well as any reminders of work or finances that might trigger stressful thoughts. Creating a peaceful sleep environment can go a long way toward nurturing deep sleep and improved energy all day long.

Meditate on the Mattress

Count slowly from ten down to one. Breathe in and out and think *ten*, breathe in and out and think *nine*. Don't let any other thought enter your mind. Don't look ahead to seven when you are still on eight. When you get to one, start over from ten.

End on a High Note

Thinking positive thoughts as you drift into sleep can help you get a better night's rest. Keep a copy of an inspirational article or a book of inspirational quotes near your bedside, and read a few pages before you turn off the light.

Grateful Dreamer

Instead of counting sheep, try counting your blessings instead. People who fall asleep focusing on gratitude sleep better and longer, and wake with a more positive outlook.

Close Your Eyes

Don't wait for nighttime to get some shut-eye. Lie down for a few minutes with an eye mask or eye pillow to shut out the light and provide gentle pressure on your eyes. Feel your thoughts slow and your mind relax into stillness.

Low Battery

During the day, when you receive a low-battery alert from your phone, laptop, or other electronic device, pause before you reach for the power cord or charger. Use this electronic message as a reminder to consider whether you, too, are running on low battery. What are some ways you can recharge your inner energy sources?

Sweet Dreams

When we lose out on sleep, we lose out on dreaming, too. This is a situation worth remedying. Science tells us that REM sleep, when most dreams take place, helps with problem solving, emotional regulation, and much more. In addition, the practice of doing dreamwork, including dream analysis and sharing dreams with a counselor or loved one, has been shown to improve relationships, heal post-traumatic stress disorder, reduce stress, and amp up creativity. To encourage dream-filled sleep and to use your dreams as a resource for increased happiness and meaning in your life, consider these suggestions.

NIGHT NOTES: Keep your journal by your bedside, and before you turn out the lights write about the highlights of the day that just passed. This helps clear your mind so you can sleep and dream better. When you wake, reach for the journal again and jot down your dreams. Recording dreams helps to increase dream recall, and helps you pay attention to the messages and information contained within your dreams.

DREAM TIME: When you wake, before you move or speak, take a moment to reflect on any dreams you might have had. There's no need to analyze or even understand them; simply review them as you would look back on an eventful day. Scan them for any information that might give you a new perspective — that might startle, amuse, entertain, or inform you.

DREAM SHARING: Make it a practice to ask your bed partner or family members about their dreams. Again, there's no need to analyze or even interpret the dreams. Simply by taking an interest in your dreams and those of your loved ones, you are inviting new opportunities to deepen your connections. As an added bonus, the process of talking out dreams sometimes sparks surprising insights.

> Night is my favorite day —
> I love silence so.
>
> **Emily Dickinson**

three

Joy at Home

Home is a name, a word,
it is a strong one;
stronger than magician ever spoke,
or spirit answered to,
in strongest conjuration.

Charles Dickens,
Martin Chuzzlewit

HOME
Is Where the Heart Is

It's one of those phrases stitched onto samplers and needlepoint pillows. It's reflexively repeated to the point where we no longer consider what we're really saying: home is where the heart is — but what does that really mean?

For starters, we are reminded that home is more than a configuration of walls, windows, doors, floors, and a roof. It isn't merely an address, and it isn't confined to a particular zip code. Home is the feeling we have when we are inside the rooms that are most familiar to us, or when we're standing beneath a star-drenched night sky. We might feel at home not in a particular place, but instead with certain people.

Sure, we can make our apartment or our house more comfortable with cozy and colorful decorations, stylish sofas, plump pillows, and eye-catching color schemes. We can fill the air with the scents of simmering stews and freshly baked fruit pies, and we can adorn our tables with hand-painted bowls and shining platters. But home is not the sum total of our possessions, either.

Home is the metaphorical equivalent of those things with which we furnish our houses. It is the feeling of kicking off our shoes and putting up our feet. It is the sense that we are nourished and delighted within our soul.

No matter what neighborhood you reside in, home is located in your spiritual heart. It is the sweet peace deep inside. Turn the key of contentment and joy, and step inside. No matter where you are, you truly are at home.

EXERCISES *for Joy at Home*

Make Room

Think of each room in your apartment or house as representing your intention to feel truly at home in your heart. Perhaps the kitchen represents your desire to nourish your soul; the living room might represent your wish to connect meaningfully with family and friends; your bedroom might represent your commitment to embracing and valuing rest and relaxation to balance and support your desire to do and achieve. Now make one change in each room that affirms your intention: add or update a piece of furniture, hang a picture that represents how you want to feel in this space, or remove objects that contradict your intention.

Love Where You Live

After browsing through magazines or watching television, it might seem as if your humble abode simply doesn't measure up to the quaint cottages, stylish condos, or magnificent mansions in the media. To fall in love with your home again, make a list of its best qualities as if you were composing a real estate ad. What are the most appealing traits about your neighborhood; about the size and layout of your home and yard? What little touches distinguish your home? Allow yourself to fall in love with your living space all over again.

Happiness Is . . .

What do you really need to be happy? Consider this question and journal your responses. Then ask again: "What do I *really* need to be happy?" Keep going until you discover the essence of what happiness means to you.

Room to Relax

You can use the same strategies for creating space in your day as you use to declutter closets and drawers. Look at your day planner or electronic calendar and notice how many items on your schedule are things you *should* do as opposed to things you *want* to do. What can you cancel or reschedule to create space for the activities that bring you joy?

Loosen Up

Just as we can hold onto objects at home and create clutter, we often hold onto emotions and create tension. Do your fingers habitually curl into fists? Are you holding on tightly to your point of view in an argument or debate? Experiment with opening up and letting go.

Precious Objects

Choose a room, or a corner of a room, and commit to decluttering it. Consider each item, and employ the adage: "Do I know this object to be useful? Do I believe it to be beautiful?" If the answer to both of these questions is no, give the item away, recycle it, or throw it away.

Before enlightenment
chop wood,
carry water.

After enlightenment
chop wood,
carry water.

Zen Saying

Chop Wood, Carry Water

CLEAN UP YOUR ROUTINE: Do an everyday activity with exquisite focus. When you sweep the floor, focus only on the motion of the broom swishing across the linoleum. If another thought intrudes, release it and return to the simple movement of your arm and the sound of the broom. Try this when performing any chore, including doing the dishes, folding laundry, wiping down countertops, or scrubbing the sink.

CHORE TIME: Repetitive tasks such as doing the dishes or folding laundry are excellent opportunities to practice bringing the mind home to our intentions, to be present, to act with love, and to be generous. As you work, practice connecting to the breath, to the present moment, and to your desire to live a more joyful and meaningful life.

TRASH TALK: Mundane tasks become more meaningful when you take a new view. As you take the trash to the curb, imagine you are letting go of old behaviors or thoughts that no longer serve you. When you weed the garden, imagine you are uprooting unnecessary mental habits from your mind, such as grudges, complaints, or regrets. When you wash dishes, feel your heart and mind being cleansed of unwanted thoughts or feelings.

On an ERRAND

You walk into the kitchen, look around, and ask yourself, "What did I come in here for?" You overhear your partner muttering in the living room, shaking his head as he scans the bookshelves, "Darn, I know I came in here for something, now what was it?" It's a common experience for people of all ages, and when we get older, it only seems to happen more often: We know we were on an errand, but we can't quite remember what it was we were looking for. Now, imagine that you've reached a ripe old age, and as you reflect on your life, the same question arises: "What did I come here for? I know I came into this life on some important errand. What was it?"

Did you come into this world to learn to love but get sidetracked by your quest to make money? Was your true mission to help and to heal, but on the way you got lost in a sea of paperwork or in an ocean of fear?

Whether you are doing chores at home or contemplating your life on a grander scale, setting intentions day to day, and even moment to moment, helps to stave off the head-shaking puzzlement about what you meant to do with the one precious life you've been granted.

EXERCISES *for Joy at Home*

A New Agenda

The day's to-do list is always at hand. It's posted on the refrigerator, typed into your smartphone, or jotted down on a square of paper and tucked into your wallet. It reminds you to pick up the dry cleaning, fill the car with gas, and take your son shopping for new shoes. Today, add to the tasks on your daily list one heart intention, such as "Breathe deeply," "Be kind," or "Be generous." Enjoy the way that adding a heart-focused task to your to-do list each day makes all the other chores you need to accomplish feel more meaningful and joyful to perform.

Rest Your Mind

Choose a cozy corner of your home and declare it to be your peaceful haven. Use pillows, candles, a string of lights, or artwork to make this an environment you will want to visit often. Whenever you come to this spot, commit to coming into the present moment, dropping your worries, and reconnecting with your joyful heart. Get comfortable and settle into the perfection of now.

Get in Touch

A shiny black stone you found on a hike and set on the desk in your study where you pay your bills can remind you of the abundance found in nature and keep you from sinking into worry about money. A bit of rose quartz beside your bed can remind you to wake each morning with your heart set on joy. A vase of fresh flowers just inside the front door might remind you to look for beauty in all your moments at home. Place a touchstone (an object that is meaningful to you) in each room to remind you of your intentions for creating a joyful and meaningful life.

There's no place like home.

L. Frank Baum, *The Wonderful Wizard of Oz*

Bless this door,
that it may prove,
Ever open,
To joy and love

Helen Taylor and May H. Brahe,
"Bless This House," lullaby

Coming HOME Again

The mezuzah, which hangs on the doorpost of many Jewish homes, can take many shapes and forms. It may be a small rectangular wooden box or a slender canister, decorated with vines and leaves, a majestic tree, or a simple house. The containers vary, but tucked inside each one is a scroll containing a prayer reminding those who walk through the doorway to hold God's teachings in their hearts and express them with the work of their hands, and in what they teach to their children.

You don't have to be Jewish or believe in God to benefit from the wisdom of this ritual object. Placing something you find meaningful or sacred at the doorpost of your home can help you keep your best intentions with you as you enter and leave, and to express those values with all your heart, with the work and touch of your hands, and with the words you speak.

EXERCISES *for Joy at Home*

Through the Door

As you prepare to leave home for the day, perform an everyday habitual task in slow motion. Put on your socks and shoes, pull on your gloves, or pick up your keys and unlock the door while paying exquisite attention to the movements and sensations of your hands. Bring this feeling of loving, mindful attention to details you normally rush past, as you continue out the door and on your way.

Homecoming

Whether it's when you are gazing into a star-filled sky, sitting in the back of a church listening to the choir sing, or standing in a museum surrounded by beautiful art, there are moments when you feel truly at home. It's that feeling that you are wrapped in infinite love and comfort — even if you are all alone. Identify the times and places that give you that feeling of deep connection, then revisit them in memory and imagination when you want to affirm and amplify your faith that all is well.

Portals into Possibility

Phones, tablets, and computers are all doorways to a world of information and communication. To help move consciously through these virtual doorways, place images on the home screens of your electronic devices that reflect the values you want to hold onto as you navigate the endless possibilities you encounter as you exchange messages and texts, and search out information and merchandise on the web.

There is no end
of craving.

Hence contentment alone
is the best way to happiness.

Therefore, acquire
contentment.

Swami Sivananda

Constant
CRAVINGS

Whether it's more food, more love, more attention, more security, more money, or even more time to relax, a great source of unhappiness is our constant craving for more. Individually and as a culture, we value consumption and growth. No wonder we have an obesity epidemic and a continual quest to find more resources — to fuel our cars and propel our national economy forward, and also to energize our personal stores of energy to keep us active and achieving. This oversized problem can be managed in bite-size increments. Meals and snacks provide perfect opportunities to practice the art of knowing when enough is enough.

EXERCISES *for Joy at Home*

Bite by Bite

Practice taking three mindful bites at the start of each meal. These first tastes of food are eaten in silence, with complete attention on the taste, texture, and aroma of your food. Notice how much more satisfying and nourishing your meal is when you begin this way.

Say Grace

Offering a prayer before a meal is a good way to affirm your intention to eat mindfully. A good phrase to add to your existing prayer, or to speak as a simple affirmation before a meal or snack, is this heartfelt wish: "May I be satisfied."

Happy Balance

Happiness is a balance between desire and satisfaction. Food is a great place to pay attention to the interplay between these forces. Notice how your body feels when you eat. Can you sense when you are sated, but not quite full? Try ending your meal there, and notice the difference in your experience when you stop eating before you've had too much.

Practice Restraint

Let others at the table help themselves to food first, while you center yourself with a calming breath and the affirmation that there is enough for all, and that you, too, will have all that you need. Allow yourself to experience the joy of anticipation while you wait for your turn to help yourself to just the right amount of food.

And forget not
that the earth delights
to feel your bare feet
and the winds long to
play with your hair.

Kahlil Gibran, *The Prophet*

Hummingbird GARDEN

A phosphorescent green comma of a bird weighing little more than a penny, the hummingbird hovers above the bright flame of a lobelia's petal while probing its depths. This little fleck of winged beauty seems to float effortlessly for the pure pleasure of it, but the hummingbird is actually hard at work. Its diminutive wings beat from 30 to 70 times per second as it extracts sugary nectar from deep inside the flowers it loves.

The hummingbird, with its determined pursuit of what is sweet and essential, makes for a fitting symbol of joy and happiness. The hummingbird reminds us that drinking in joy is not a passive pursuit. Hummingbirds use all their physical powers and tricks to achieve their goals. They fly forward and backward, and even upside down, in their quest for the best of what life has to offer.

We can learn how to live more joyfully by observing the hummingbird. This little bird reminds us to seek out joy with grace and ease, to bring color into our lives, and to effect a lightness of spirit in all we do.

EXERCISES *for Joy at Home*

Fountain of Joy

A small electric fountain can be added to an arrangement of potted plants indoors or your garden outside. Falling water adds negative ions to the environment, which are said to make us feel happier, reduce irritation, and have a positive impact on mild forms of depression.

Bloom

Pick a bouquet of wildflowers, or buy a few stems from your local florist. Fresh flowers in your home invite you to contemplate beauty and the abundance of nature. Gazing at plants can also help you relax.

Invite Joy

Plant lobelia, rose of Sharon, bee balm, or lupine in your garden to attract hummingbirds. Bask in the simple delight of seeing these colorful birds, and let them remind you to prioritize the pursuit of joy.

How Sweet It Is

How can you bring more sweetness into your life? Reflect on this question in your journal and make a list of everyday delights that are like nectar for you. (Think metaphorically here . . . relying on sweet foods for happiness can lead to new problems!)

Grow Your Joy

Working in the garden reduces stress, increases happiness, and even helps people sleep better. Create a small garden in your yard, or on your windowsill, rooftop, or terrace. Spend a little time each day tending to plants and watch your happiness grow.

Real Beauty

Beauty is an antidote to grief and sadness. Seek out beauty when you are out and about, and adorn your home and garden with colors and objects that are pleasing to you.

four

Joy at
Work

Let the beauty
of what you love
be what you do.

Rumi

When You GROW UP

When you were hardly old enough to write your name, Old Aunt So-and-So started in with The Question: "What do you want to be when you grow up?" In response, you plucked dreams from the air: astronaut, ballerina, firefighter, doctor, fairy princess. Back then, you were a pint-sized packet of potential, standing on tiptoe to make your small voice heard over the horizon of the dining room table as you told all those curious adults gathered for a holiday feast about your biggest dreams.

The question was in fact an invitation. It was your cue to dream up ways you would one day bedazzle the world. Your answers were promises to your future self that one day you would rocket, twirl, race, ride, cure, or create. You played at dress-up and tried on various identities. You imagined adventures, not stock portfolios or benefit packages; you would discover new planets, wow audiences, sing songs, or clean up oceans. You knew something as a child, but perhaps forgot it as an adult. Your job is to blossom, grow, heal, learn, teach, and inspire. Sure, there would be a paycheck, but first there would be exciting exploits; there would be daring deeds and inquiries fueled by curiosity and interest.

Think back to your answer to the long-ago question. Can you connect the dots between the 4-year-old you who blurted a dream when asked what you wanted to be — and the grown person holding this book right now? If not, how can you reconnect with some of the qualities of your long-ago aspirations?

EXERCISES *for Joy at Work*

Work It Out

If you always wanted to be an artist but now you are a lawyer, can you sign up for a painting class? If you dreamed of owning a dude ranch but now you work in insurance, can you visit a stable and commune with the horses? Take a small, symbolic, or significant step to reconnect with your dreams.

Net Worth

You can increase the true worthiness of your work today by shifting your focus to the things you value most. Make a list of what you truly value about the work you do — reflect on your job, your coworkers, clients, and products.

Making a Life — or a Living

According to ancient Indian religions such as Buddhism and Hinduism, each person has her own dharma to fulfill in life. *Dharma*, a Sanskrit word, means "right way of living." Can you connect what you do to make a living with the core values you associate with "living right"? Write down the three things you value most, and consider ways you can bring one of those qualities into your workday.

Follow Your Bliss

What do you love to do? Anything goes: cooking, eating, dressing up for costume parties, telling your daughter a bedtime story, working in the garden. Consider your answers to this question. Are there any common themes, skills, or qualities — such as caring, creating, communicating — that connect some of these activities? If so, can you incorporate those skills and qualities in the work you do? Is there a job or volunteer opportunity you'd like to aim for in the future that would bring you in line with doing some of the things you love?

MODERN *Times*

The image of Charlie Chaplin as The Little Tramp in the iconic film *Modern Times* may seem quaint now, but the accelerated pace of work and our desperate attempts to keep up are not so different now from what they were in the Industrial Age that is comically portrayed in that classic film. In fact, as technology improves, it seems more difficult than ever to foster a healthy relationship with time and to resist the ever-growing pressures to produce more and more at absurdly escalating rates of speed.

In addition, technology has caused a blurring of lines between work time and personal time. The Internet tempts us into distractions during the workday, and smartphones and electronic tablets set up the expectation that we will be available around the clock for business.

Ancient wisdom, however, provides the antidote for the frantic pace of our lives in these modern times. The Sabbath, a time-honored call to refrain from worldly pursuits one day a week, is still something we can adapt to our harried lives. In addition, meditative and contemplative traditions from various faiths teach us to quiet our minds and find a timeless realm of peace and serenity within, no matter what is happening in the world around us.

It is our challenge then to combine today's technology with ancient wisdom to help us use the gift of time consciously and to set priorities that support and strengthen our intentions.

EXERCISES *for Joy at Work*

Break Time

Take brief breaks every 45 minutes at work. Frequent short breaks have been proven to increase productivity. They make you feel good, too. So set an alert to remind you to get up, gaze out the window, or make a cup of calming herbal tea at regular intervals.

Anytime Sabbath

Whether you can allocate time for an entire day of rest or not, you can create Sabbath space in your life by turning off your phone, unplugging the modem, or saying no to "shoulds" for a specified time each day or week. Use this time to connect to your heart, to nature, or to silence — and create space for joy to flow into.

Slow the Flow

Emails and texts speed up our communications to the point where we can barely keep up some days. You can take control of the pace of your life by pausing before your reply. Take three breaths, three hours, or even three days before answering most messages. Better yet, if time permits, respond with a phone call, or even a postcard dropped in the mail.

To see a world
in a grain of sand
And a heaven
in a wild flower,
Hold infinity
in the palm of your hand,
And eternity
in an hour.

William Blake,
"Auguries of Innocence"

Separation of Work and Home

Use separate email accounts for personal and work contacts. When at work, resist the temptation to check personal emails, and when at home, resist the urge to check work messages. You can also designate different ringtones for work contacts and personal contacts so you'll be alerted as to whether it's your work or home life calling before you reach for your phone.

Wristwatch

The wristwatch is a disappearing fashion accessory, as people increasingly opt to check their smartphones for the time instead. But glancing at an electronic screen reveals more than just the time of day. When looking to our phones for the time, we're bombarded by email alerts, text messages, and news headlines. Looking to your wristwatch or wall clock instead calms the inflow of information. Technology might dictate trends, but peace of mind never goes out of fashion.

Explore daily
the will of God.

Carl G. Jung

A New BOTTOM LINE

No matter how healthy your paycheck, even the highest salary is never enough to buy true happiness. In fact, young Americans today say that having meaningful work is their top career priority. And you don't have to forgo a robust income to find deeply satisfying work. Volunteering, joining the Peace Corps, and working for a nonprofit are traditional ways to find meaningful work — but those aren't the only ways. Infusing a sense of meaning into what you already do day to day and moment by moment, in whatever position you hold, is the real key to finding a joyful sense of purpose at work.

For today, focus on how you accomplish your work rather than how much you accomplish. Ask yourself how you can increase your sense of engagement at work. Perhaps you can bring authentic communication and meaningful connection to the next phone call you make or the next email you compose. Even if you work in an environment where people are overworked and underpaid, you can find ways to be generous in spirit with yourself and your coworkers. Offer compliments or a helping hand. Be creative as you consider ways to increase the value of your experience and bring moments of stillness and calm into your mind and heart as you go about your business.

EXERCISES *for Joy at Work*

The Company You Keep

You might spend more time with your coworkers than with family members. Consider the people you work with and look for one collegial relationship that needs a boost. Commit to doing one thing to nurture or improve that connection this week. You might ask this person how her day is going and really listen to her answer; tell her what you appreciate about her work; or bring her a cup of coffee or tea.

How Was Your Day, Dear?

Don't wait until the end of the day to evaluate how it went. Ask yourself at least three times between clocking in and clocking out how you are experiencing your day so far. If the day is dragging on, call to mind an instance where you or someone around you displayed kindness or caring, give yourself a hand and wrist massage, or see if you can make someone laugh.

Who's the Boss?

Whatever your job description might say, your true purpose at work is yours to determine. It could be anything from connecting with others to creating calm or easing the suffering of those around you by offering small acts of loving-kindness, humor, or understanding. Today, take on the job of creating a new, heart-centered job description for yourself.

Top-Down Management

Each time you end a phone call or prepare to begin a meeting, do a quick scan of your face and head. Close your eyes and bring attention to your scalp, forehead, lips, jaw, and neck. Imagine each area softening like butter on a warm stove as you relax and release any tension that has accumulated in your body.

Technology is nothing.
What's important is that
you have a faith in people,
that they're basically
good and smart,
and if you give them tools,
they'll do wonderful
things with them.

Steve Jobs

KEY*boarding*

Remember when you were a child and you gathered with your friends around a Ouija board? You rested your fingers on the sliding planchette as it roved over the letters and numbers on the board to reveal answers to your deepest questions. Sometimes the computer feels like just such a magical device: place your fingers on the keyboard and ask a question — anything from what is the size of a dog's brain, to how to prepare chicken cacciatore, to what the weather will be on your upcoming wedding day — and the answers appear within moments. We strike the right combination of computer keys and we're connected with sites where we can find love, jobs, inspirational lectures, and communities of like-minded people who might live oceans away.

It's easy to gripe about technology. We bemoan the time we waste on the latest social media site, or how easily we fall into a trance of skipping through various links to view videos or read blog posts that steal our time rather than enrich our lives. But there's no denying that the Internet can also open us to a powerful universe of information, advice, and connection — if we use it consciously.

Today, when you rest your fingers on your computer keyboard, remind yourself that you have the opportunity to tap into a world of opportunity and possibility. By setting an intention and checking in with it again and again as you navigate through cyberspace, you can use technology to support you in learning, growing, creating, and becoming your best self.

EXERCISES *for Joy at Work*

Key Words

Infuse the vocabulary of your keyboard with meaning. Let the SHIFT key remind you to shift into a joyful attitude. Let the ESC key remind you to commit to Extreme Self Care. When you hit the @ key, use it to remind you to check in with where you are at in this moment — breathe in and connect to your body and your heart.

PIN Meaning to It

Every time you go to the ATM, or access your money over the Internet or through a telephone banking system, you need to key in a set of characters. When you set your PINs and passwords, choose letter and number combinations that help you keep focused on your intentions. Try LTN247 if you want to remember to Love Thy Neighbor 24 hours, 7 days a week, or J0y2d@y, L0vlngklndne55, or any other creative combination that works for you.

Time Study

Time-tracking apps can help you chart how you use your time by giving you a graphic depiction of whether you are sticking to your priorities or wandering off course. Other apps can block websites you can't seem to stop checking, or even prevent you from browsing the Internet for certain periods of time throughout the day. Choose an app or program that will help you manage your time on- and off-line well.

Sticky Note

Place a sticky note over the power button on your computer with a message such as "Intentions first" that will remind you to prioritize your goals before you log in.

My desk drawer
is filled with all kinds
of prayers.

Geraldine Ferraro

Desk JOB

Once it held an inkpot, blotter, and quill pen. Today it may hold a phone, a computer, a disc drive, and a tangle of power cords. It may be in a study or a cubicle, at home or in an office building. Your desk may be a simple wooden table or an ergonomic wonder. Likely it is the place where you budget, spend, plan, and communicate. It provides a surface where you can spread out papers, stack files, and store supplies. Often a desk is a utilitarian place for paying bills and filing papers — but it can also be the place from which you launch your best ideas, create, produce, plan, and imagine new solutions.

If you work at a desk inputting data, answering phones, or running a department or a company, chances are you have strong feelings about this bit of work-a-day real estate. A desk job can be a symbol of longed-for stability or dreaded stasis. "I don't want to live my life behind a desk" is a common refrain. When we say that, we mean we want to know our time is our own, and that we're not shackled to someone else's schedule.

At the same time, the desk is one area that most workers have some control over. Whether telecommuting from home or working in a cubicle at a large company, people often assert their individuality at their desks by displaying quotes, comics, and pictures meant to amuse, inspire, or distract. Your desk or work area also reveals things you may not have realized you were projecting about how you feel about the work you do, as well as the attitude you bring to it.

Is your desk a place you avoid or a place you are drawn to? What steps can you take to make your work environment one that reflects and reinforces your true values about the work you do?

EXERCISES *for Joy at Work*

Clear Your Desk

There is a difference between creative chaos and claustrophobic clutter. Remove three things from your desk that are unnecessary or unappealing.

Take Note

What is on your desk; what is around it? Do these objects inspire or distract? Pick up a pad and paper and take note. What message does your work area broadcast about your feelings about work and your work style? Commit to one action you can take this week to make your desk a more inviting environment.

A New Light

Salt lamps are said to release negative ions that boost moods and neutralize the detrimental magnetic fields emitted by computer monitors and other electronic devices. Try plugging one in beside your computer and enjoy the soothing glow, as well as the possible health benefits.

Desk Totem

Shop for some small item to keep on your desk or hang above it that will remind you of the spirit you want to bring to your work. It might be a colorful toy, puppet, stuffed animal, painting, or plant.

Pencil Tip

Instead of tucking a pencil behind your ear, try placing it between your teeth. Holding a pencil in your mouth forces you to lift your lips into a smile, thus elevating your mood. (Yes, science has proven that the act of smiling, in and of itself, makes us happier.)

Body of Work

These are simple exercises you can practice at work that will help you feel better and won't require a change of clothes or special mat.

OFFICE CHAIR: A modified forward bend can calm your mind. Stand with your feet shoulder-width apart, a couple of feet from the back of a chair. With your hands on your hips, exhale and bend forward from the hips. Grab your elbows with your hands and rest your arms on top of the chair back, placing your forehead on your arms. Keep your feet parallel and your knees relaxed and not locked. Feel supported by the strength in your legs as you let your spine relax and the muscles in your face and neck soften. Breathe easily. When you are ready to stand again, feel your feet firmly rooted on the floor, inhale, and lift to a standing position from the strength in your legs.

LEAN IN: To counteract the stressful effects of hunching forward at your computer, place your hands on either side of a doorway and lean forward, gently stretching your chest and shoulders.

OPEN UP: To undo the effects of too much typing and to open space in your heart, try this: roll your shoulders back and down, feeling your shoulder blades slide toward one another. Inhale deeply, and feel the increased confidence and sense of expansiveness this creates.

Made of MONEY

Can money buy happiness? To an extent, yes. Studies have shown that people are happier once they have enough wealth to cover their basic needs. But after that, increases in income do not correlate with increases in happiness. Yet the way we throw ourselves into working more and more hours at jobs with increasingly high stress levels, you would think that true happiness depends on clawing our way to the highest tax bracket possible.

By shifting your thoughts about money, however, you can exchange some of your anxiety for serenity. For example, observe the inner chatter that plays in your head as you pay bills, shop for clothes, or evaluate your budget. Notice the words you use when you talk to family or friends about whether you can afford to take a vacation, buy a new car, or donate to a charity. All too often when people talk about money they talk about lack of it, or about the troubles it causes in life. Just look at common expressions about money to see how our culture primes us to equate money with stress: "Dirty money." "Money is the root of all evil." "A day late and a dollar short."

But as with everything else, you can choose. You can shift how you think about, and what you say about, money — and buy a little more happiness in the bargain.

EXERCISES *for Joy at Work*

Currency

The word *currency* means "flow." Are you damming up the flow of money in your life with thoughts of not having enough? Today, trust that the natural inflow and outflow of resources will provide you with all that you need and will allow you to give all that is good.

Meditate on Enough

Imagine that you have plenty of money to meet all your needs and more. Imagine that your bank account is robust and you can provide for yourself and your loved ones, and have more left over. How does it feel? How do you sit when you have plenty? How do you walk? What expression do you wear on your face? Breathe it in. Now open your eyes and take this feeling into your day.

Spending Budget

Allot a certain amount of money each week to spend on things that bring you joy. Even a modest sum will buy a little whimsy. For just a few dollars you can download some uplifting songs, buy a special treat at the French bakery you usually rush past, or buy a glitter pen. Get creative . . . and get spending.

Money can't buy me love.

The Beatles,
"Can't Buy Me Love"

Count Your Change

When you count your change or throw a few quarters in a tip jar, use the jangling sound of coins clinking together as your reminder to exchange a negative thought for a positive one.

The Price of Connection

List all the ways you do use or could use your money to help you connect with others: buying someone dinner, donating to a charity that helps diminish people's suffering, increasing another person's wealth by paying them for goods or services you value, and so on. Viewing money as a currency for connection will help you set priorities for how you allocate your resources — and it may even make you smile as you spend.

Withholding Tax

Not only do we get caught in the myth that more money will make us happier, but we sometimes fret over every penny we spend. We clip coupons, compare prices at the gas pump, and bargain with sales clerks to save a few bucks. We spend so much energy on saving that we forget that generosity breeds joy. Today, give away a little — buy a cup of coffee for the person behind you in line, throw a few bucks in the hat for the busker in the subway station, or buy yourself flowers.

Getting over Overwhelm

When you need to get out from under a tidal wave of deadlines, the first step is to tame your breath. Calming your breath allows you to think clearly and access creative solutions. Try this 4-7-8 breathing technique, which is an effective antidote to anxiety:

1. Exhale completely through your mouth.

2. Close your mouth, and inhale deeply through your nose to the count of 4.

3. Gently hold your breath to the count of 7.

4. Exhale through your open mouth for the count of 8.

5. Repeat steps 2 through 4 for about four cycles twice a day as needed. Keep your counting rhythm consistent, and most of all, be gentle with yourself. Return to normal breathing anytime the exercise feels too difficult, or if you begin to feel lightheaded.

five

Joy on the Go

We travel, initially,
to lose ourselves;
and we travel, next,
to find ourselves.

Pico Iyer

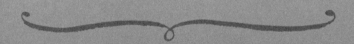

Destination
UNKNOWN

You studied the maps, tour books, and travel sites for weeks before setting out on this trip. You bookmarked the museums you planned to visit and the sites you wanted most to see. But on the first day of your journey, en route to a grand statue you looked forward to seeing, you get lost amongst the other tourists weighted down by their cameras, plastic water bottles, and maps. You make a wrong turn and stumble onto a lonely path along the sea, pass a fort you don't know the name of and a plaza you don't recognize from your studies of this city. You can't remember any of the foreign phrases you had memorized before you left.

Too tired to even look at the guidebook once more, you wander through tunnels and over footbridges until, feet sore and throat parched, you enter a little restaurant where you are seated on an outdoor patio in a walled garden. You look up to see an old, proud tree that is decorated with wooden birds dancing from its branches. A coil of white lights swirls around its wide trunk, creating a cheerful glow as the afternoon slips into evening. You order a drink and gaze at a little girl running between the tables with cloth roses pinned to the skirt of her bright yellow dress. A stray cat brushes its tail against your chair, peering up at you with elegant and expressive eyes. You feed it a bit of your bread, and suddenly you no longer mind that you never found that statue. You can't imagine being more content than you are right here, in the magical garden of an ordinary restaurant you weren't even looking for.

We plan and plot our happily-ever-afters: the house, the spouse, the number of children, and the career that we think will bring fulfillment. And then other things happen. If only we could accept them with the grace and ease we so easily find when we're on vacation — when disappointments are easily remedied by the small delights that couldn't be predicted by any tourist website or travel book.

Sure, it's good to scope out the territory ahead of the journey and draft a plan. But it's just as important to recognize when we're lost, ask for guidance, and allow unexpected twists and turns to bring different treasures from the ones we'd planned for. When we welcome surprises and become willing to greet the path we've landed on with a happy heart, we stumble into magic, beauty, and joy.

EXERCISES *for Joy on the Go*

Get Lost

Plan a day trip to a nearby town or city. Let yourself wander, follow your curiosity, and welcome the opportunity to get lost and stumble upon the unexpected.

Postcard from Home

When we go away on vacation, we pick up seashells or purchase little gifts to remind us of the pleasures we experienced. What little memory would you hold onto from this ordinary day? What surprise, smile, or kind word can you bring home into your heart? Write it down, and savor it.

Be a Tourist — at Home

Go through your day as if you were seeing your surroundings through the eyes of a visitor. What small delights do you pass by each day and forget to notice?

Looking Forward

In English we have a word for anticipating with dread (foreboding) but not a word for anticipating with joy. In German the word is *vorfreude* (vor-FROY-dah), and it's worth learning. People who anticipate vacations and special events tend to be happier overall. So enjoy looking forward, whether you have a vacation planned or not. Each evening, make a list of three things you are looking forward to about the next day. Then take a few moments to practice *vorfreude*, and joyfully anticipate the pleasures to come.

Where Are You Going?

Whether you're setting out on a business trip or a two-week vacation, each journey begins with a plan. We map our routes and make rough or rigid itineraries for when we plan to leave, to arrive, and to depart again. Likewise, on life's journey we can let events take us where they may — or we can set our intentions and make a plan to fulfill them. When envisioning a direction for your life, consider not only what you want to achieve outwardly but also the inner qualities you want to bring to your life.

A good place to begin is at the end. Picture yourself as an elderly person nearing the end of life. From this perspective, consider what experiences you would have regretted not having had. What treasures would you have most appreciated? What qualities would you value having embodied?

Once you have a vision for the quality of life you want to live, set your intentions and make your best dreams come true. This Practical Visualization can help you get there.

1. Get quiet and clear your mind so that you can tap into your true nature. Allow your intention to emerge from this calm, connected place.

2. Visualize your goal as if it's already happening. Don't just *see* it but also *feel* the emotions of living this outcome. Hold this vision and feeling in your heart and mind for at least 2 minutes.

3. Now make a list of three action steps you can to take to bring this vision to fulfillment.

Happiness cannot be pursued; it must ensue.

Viktor Frankl

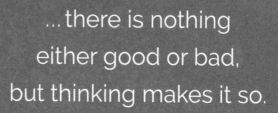

...there is nothing
either good or bad,
but thinking makes it so.

William Shakespeare, *Hamlet*

The **ROAD** *You're On*

Dorothy's yellow brick road, Hansel and Gretel's bread crumb trail, Odysseus's voyage — the stories we tell are filled with trials, triumphs, and the trails we travel as we encounter them. These stories teach us that where we come from guides us to where we're going, and that no matter how far afield we journey, we are always rooted in thoughts of home. These stories also teach us that destination is not the end of the story: the path itself is full of lessons and delight.

In her book *Wild,* about her solo hike along the Pacific Coast Trail, author Cheryl Strayed describes what she calls trail magic: ". . . the unexpected and sweet happenings that stand out in stark relief to the challenges of the trail." This concept aptly incorporates roadblocks and stumbling blocks, obstacles and detours, into the making of our most treasured adventures.

You can look for trail magic every day, whether you're lacing up your hiking boots and exploring a faraway mountain range or putting on your heels and heading to the office. Wherever you roam, be on the lookout for the sweet surprises, marvelous moments, and little drops of joy along the way.

EXERCISES *for Joy on the Go*

The View from the Stars

Stop for a moment and look up to the sky. Let your mind relax into awareness of infinite open space. Release your worries and concerns into this vast openness and watch your woes dissolve.

In Sync

Approach today as a treasure hunt. Be on the lookout for coincidences and unusual encounters. Working with synchronicity in this way helps you be in conversation with the world around you and can help you feel connected to it wherever you go.

Your Internal GPS

Wouldn't it be nice to have a GPS device that maps your path to happiness? Intuition is just that. It's the deep knowing that you feel in your body as a "gut reaction," or as a strong emotional pull. You can develop your intuition by paying attention to dreams, working with synchronicity, and spending time each day in a state of receptive silence.

Guided Journey

Use the *chin* mudra (a symbolic hand position) to help you connect with your inner guidance. Sit comfortably and quietly. Rest your hands on your thighs, palms facing up. Make an *O* shape by resting the tip of your thumb on the fingernail of your index finger. Relax and take five slow, deep breaths. Sink into a sense of still, silent expansiveness as you open your mind to your deepest knowing.

The (Active) Pursuit of Happiness

Feeling good is not a spectator sport. Search out the good in every situation. Keep peeling back the layers . . . even if it's not obvious at first, the good is in there someplace!

WALK *This Way*

You take a stroll through your neighborhood in the evening as daylight fades and houselights twinkle on. You meander along a path through meadows where great blue herons nest in the springtime and late afternoon sunlight turns the fields to gold in autumn. Or perhaps you power-walk the perimeter of an urban park. Whatever landscape you walk through, your mood will likely improve by the time you return home.

Doctors tell us walking is good for the heart, and philosophers tell us it is good for the soul. We know that walking is an antidote for everything from high blood pressure to low moods. According to Chinese medicine, the very act of walking gently massages pressure points on the bottoms of our feet that alleviate depression, thus making us feel better through and through.

Walking also allows us to experience the world at a human pace — the pace that fits our stride and allows us to intimately connect with our environment as we go. Walking is a luxurious bath for the senses, and a balm to the spirit.

A half hour's walk a day, alone or with a friend, is all it takes to bring a little more joy to our lives — and promote good health in the bargain.

EXERCISES *for Joy on the Go*

Every Step You Take

Whether you're walking across your living room or across town, consciously slow your footsteps and pay attention to each sensation as your heel, the sole of your foot, the ball of your foot, and then your toes make contact with the ground before releasing into your next step. Notice how this simple walking meditation relaxes your stride and your breath as your attention settles into the fullness of the moment as you go on your way.

Watch Your Thoughts as You Walk

Can you see a tree, a car, or another person, without internally labeling or commenting on it? Practice moving through your surroundings without attaching thoughts, stories, or judgments to what you see. Notice the sense of peace and wellness that comes with nonjudgmental being.

Portable Party

Put on your music and skip down the street to a beat. Dance walking puts a song in your heart and a swing in your hips . . . literally . . . as you move. Let others wonder what has made you so happy — or better yet, invite them to join in the fun.

Exercise Your Heart

The best exercise is the one you love doing — whether it be bicycle riding, skating, dancing, walking, jogging, rowing, swimming, or playing tennis. Find an aerobic activity that brings you pleasure and that you can joyfully commit to doing for half an hour or more each day.

Walk for a Purpose

Joining a walk to benefit people with Alzheimer's disease, autism, breast cancer, or any other cause not only allows you to get the benefit of movement and exercise, it helps you connect with others who care about the same issues you do and allows you the opportunity to generously and visibly offer your support to others.

Jump for Joy

Put a hop, skip, or jump into your step. Not only is it fun, but jumping and hopping also help build strong bones.

Ear Candy

Make a playlist of happy songs. This isn't necessarily music that makes you feel hip, smart, cultured, or countercultural. These are the songs that make you tap your foot, shake your hips, get silly, and sing along — even if you can't carry a tune. This will be your go-to list when you want to jump-start the happy in your day.

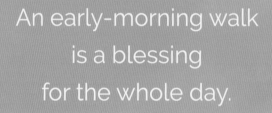

An early-morning walk
is a blessing
for the whole day.

Henry David Thoreau

Roadblock

Detours and obstacles slow us down whether we like it or not. Next time you encounter a roadblock — literal or figurative — view the obstacle as an opportunity to practice resilience or equanimity. Take a long, slow breath; regroup; and consider the gifts in the unexpected twists and turns your day has taken.

SPEED LIMIT: When you zoom down the highway and notice a state trooper's car tucked into a curve with a radar gun pointed your way, rather than feeling annoyed, say a silent thank-you to that trooper as you ease your foot off the accelerator. Let speed limit signs and the officers who enforce them act as reminders to fully inhabit the present, rather than rush ahead to the next destination.

THE STONES IN THE ROAD: The most formidable obstacles we face are the negative stories we tell ourselves about our circumstances — as opposed to the circumstances themselves. List any limiting beliefs that keep you from fully experiencing happiness, joy, and self-fulfillment. Explore these thoughts through journal writing or talking with a trusted friend or trained therapist.

STOPLIGHT SCAN: When you come to a stoplight, take the opportunity to mentally scan your body from head to toe, noticing and releasing any tense muscles as you go.

In today's rush
we all think too much,
seek too much, want too much
and forget about the joy
of just Being.

Eckhart Tolle,
The Power of Now

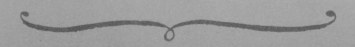

Don't Go It ALONE

You step into the subway station on a morning when even deciphering your route to a new part of the city feels like too much work. So rather than refer to the colorful map posted on the platform, you ask a stranger for directions. She is heading in the same direction and offers to help you find your stop. As you begin to talk she tells you that she is in town to care for a sick sister. You tell her you know how she feels, as you've been caring for your ailing mother. Suddenly you are seated side by side, swapping stories and offering each other comfort. It's as though the subway car has become your personal support group, and when the train pulls into your stop you emerge from it having experienced true connection.

Perhaps we've taken too much to heart those childhood warnings not to talk to strangers. We work hard to avoid another's gaze, let alone talk to them. In fact, research has shown that most people believe that sitting alone on a train or subway will make the ride more pleasant — and we see evidence of it all around. On crowded buses and trains, people use earbuds to cocoon themselves away with their own music, or they crouch over their smartphones surfing the web, or they browse titles on their tablets — all while studiously ignoring their seatmates. But research has also shown that people who talk to a stranger on their commute are happier, proving that casual social contact lifts our spirits. So next time you're on your morning commute, remove your earbuds and make conversation — and see if a chance encounter boosts your mood.

EXERCISES *for Joy on the Go*

Let a Smile Be Your Companion

Whether you are walking to the bus stop or seated on the subway, offer a smile to everyone you meet. Smiling not only makes you feel better — it's also a gift to the recipient.

The Kindness of Strangers

Offer to help someone carry her bags, give your seat to someone who might need it more than you do, or hold open the door for someone who has his hands full. Look for three ways to be kind to strangers today, and bask in the glow of connection.

Pleasant Journey

Appreciate the simple pleasures when you are out and about — the sound of a sonata streaming from your radio, the taste of a cream-filled pastry, the scent of lilacs wafting on the spring breeze. Then take a moment to wish this pleasure on someone you know who is suffering.

Love on the Move

Metta meditation is a simple practice in which you offer loving-kindness first to yourself, then to others. You can try this seated on a cushion or on the go. Next time you are walking on a crowded city street or standing in line to board a train or plane, try offering a simple wish for love and kindness to yourself, and then to everyone you see. Simply repeat to yourself: "May I be happy, may she be happy. May I be happy, may he be happy," as you continue to encounter others. (See page 186 for a longer metta meditation exercise.)

Stop
chasing your dreams.
Allow them to come
to you in perfect order with
unquestioned timing.
Slow down
your frantic pace . . .

Wayne Dyer,
Change Your Thoughts — Change Your Life

SLOW *Going*

The hub of a wheel. The eye of a tornado. In the midst of movement there is stillness. Likewise, there is stillness deep inside you, even as you bustle about, meeting deadlines and getting things done. A joyful life depends on honoring this dynamic tension between being and doing. We can take action to create the conditions that support a more joyful life, but we must also know when to let go and surrender to stillness to allow the good to simply emerge.

You can't chase joy, control it, or grab onto it. By slowing down and getting comfortable with quiet, we allow joy to rise from within us and effortlessly brighten our days.

You can use repeated words (mantras), conscious breathing, and creative reminders to slow down, get in touch with your calm center, and return again to your intentions — even on the busiest day.

EXERCISES *for Joy on the Go*

Slow Lane

Decide to drive in the right lane today. Let this commitment to forgoing speed remind you to slow down your thoughts, as well as your pace, all day long.

Speed Limit

Slow Down for Smiles. Joy Zone 5 mph. Time Passing: Proceed with Care. Create a whimsical Speed Limit sign and post it on your dashboard, at your desk, or over the sink in your bathroom or kitchen. Let it make you smile as you downshift into a slower gear.

Attitude Shift

When you shift gears as you drive, decide to make a subtle shift to your attitude as well. For example, shift from "What do I want to do today?" to "How do I want to experience my life today?" Shift from "Why me?" to "Given that this is happening, who do I want to be in response?"

Word for the Wise

Try using a word such as *stillness, silence, spaciousness,* or *joy* as your mantra today. Say the word silently to yourself when you are waiting in line or pausing between tasks, or any time you notice your mind wandering to stressful thoughts.

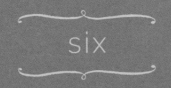

six

Joy in Solitude

Loneliness
is the poverty
of self;
solitude
is the richness
of self.

May Sarton

Wake to SOLITUDE

The streetlights have winked off and the electric lights have not yet flickered on in neighboring houses. Before your eyes even open, you sense the peach glow of early sun on your bare arms and shoulders — and for a moment it seems as if the rays tickling you awake are yours alone. This sweet stillness is so unexpected, the delight so complete, that you hold your breath in the childlike hope that time will stand still so that this moment will never end.

This nectar-drenched pleasure is even more surprising because you realize now all the ways you avoid being quiet and alone like this. You surround yourself with music, television, and conversation. You blot out solitude with movement, people, plans, and activity. Those half-buried dreaded fears of school cafeteria lunches — the embarrassment of having to sit alone with a plastic tray and a stack of textbooks — has never quite been exiled from the farthest reaches of your mind. Alone is dangerously close to lonely, with feelings of discomfort and unmasked pain, and so you steer clear of being by yourself whenever you can.

If you avoid being alone, you are in good company. Studies have shown that people would rather administer electric shocks to themselves than spend 15 minutes alone with their own thoughts. But forgoing time for self-reflection inhibits our ability to feel empathy and experience the full richness of life.

We are social creatures by nature, and we innately fear exclusion, expulsion, and exile. But we are soulful beings as well, and encounters with our solitary selves remind us that this way of being is nourishing and necessary — and it mustn't be neglected.

Simple quiet is an increasingly rare commodity, as electronic alerts and tones jostle us from reverie and constantly coax us to worlds of casual connection and social chatter. Yet a balance between social time and solo experience is essential to a life of meaning and joy.

Cultivating a space for inner quiet requires some focus and attention, not to mention practice. With a little effort we can find ways to connect to the inner worlds of imagination, contemplation, meditation, and soulful inquiry.

EXERCISES *for Joy in Solitude*

Solitaire

Being alone means spending time connected with your Self. It might be in the tub with candlelight or a good book, or it might be riding your bike on a country road or simply closing your eyes and listening to classical music. Consider ways that you already incorporate time alone into your life and how you can make that time even more special.

Disconnect to Connect

For at least 20 minutes a day, power off your devices (including anything with a screen or keyboard), and tune in to your inner world. Read a poem. Watch a squirrel scurry along a branch outside the window. Listen to music with no words. Let your mind wander.

Solitude in a Snap

Get in touch with solitude in nearly any situation by closing your eyes and taking one deep inhale and slow exhale while you still your thoughts and quiet your mind.

In It Alone — Together

The next time you face a challenge, think of the people in your life who inspire you. Imagine them surrounding you with love and encouragement. Now face the task at hand feeling empowered by the strengths, skills, and wisdom of the ones you love most.

Ask and You Shall Receive

Prayer is the active side of meditation. Once you've gotten still and quiet inside your mind, it's time to introduce words and images that represent your heart's deepest desire. Creating a prayer collage is an inspiring way to visualize and articulate your heart's yearning.

1. Sit quietly and get in touch with your heart's true desire.

2. Take no more than 20 minutes to flip through magazines and snip out images that represent what your dream looks and feels like. Setting a timer for just 20 minutes prevents you from overthinking your choices, thus allowing your intuitive self to take over.

3. Arrange the images you've selected on a large piece of colorful fabric or paper.

4. Keep moving the images around until the design is pleasing to you. Again, don't overthink. Instead, feel your way into a satisfying arrangement.

5. Spend several minutes in silence contemplating your prayer collage, experiencing the hopefulness and joy of seeing your dreams arrayed before you.

6. Focus now on one image at a time, and articulate aloud why it's in your collage and what aspect of your dream it represents. Direct this prayer to God, the Universe, or the powers of love and abundance in whatever form they take for you.

7. Now disassemble your collage. This is a symbolic gesture of faith and trust as you release your prayer and allow your wishes to materialize in your life in the form you imagined — or as something even better.

Keep a JOURNAL
and Journey to Your Best Self

Some people have collections of diaries that stand at attention in neat rows on shelves, ticking off the years, book by book. Others write in a ragtag collection of hardbound artist sketchbooks or whatever blank book they've come across: pocket-size to over-size, hardbacked, hand-stitched, spiral-bound, cloth-covered, or sticker-decorated. When it comes to keeping a diary or journal, commitment to process is far more important than an attractive cover or elegant prose. The trick is to find a journal-writing method that supports your exploration of the ever-evolving life you're living.

Over time, your journal becomes a guidebook to help you track your experiences and learn from them. When you dip back into past volumes, you notice patterns, make connections, and see meaning in what might otherwise be dimly recalled as a messy tangle of events. The lines of handwritten or typed text become like bread crumb trails that can lead you back home to your heart.

Whether you are an experienced journal keeper or you are just testing the waters, picking up a notebook and putting your thoughts on paper can help you deepen your experience on the page — and off.

What I feel most
is that because I am open
and available, the universe
— the idea —
comes to me. It feels a
little like being called.

Toni Morrison,
on writing

EXERCISES *for Joy in Solitude*

Pick Up a Pen

The most important thing about keeping a journal is to stick with it. Start with a reasonable goal: writing for 10 minutes a day for 21 days is a good place to start.

Be Your Own BFF

Writing in your journal is like having a conversation with your very best self. So listen to what you are saying on the page with compassion and curiosity. Receive your own words with love and patience, being present the way you would want to be for your very best friend, and the way you'd want her to be for you.

Make Your Journal a "Joynal"

In the morning, ask yourself, "What does joy look like?" Then as you go about your day, notice images, impressions, and people that exemplify joy to you. In the evening, open your journal and paste in pictures, sketch a scene, transcribe a quote, or describe in detail a moment from your day that represents one or more of the visions of joy you collected.

Bliss Now

Try this writing prompt in your journal:

1. Fill in the blanks:

   "If I already had what I'm looking for I'd be _____,
   I'd do _____, I'd feel _____."

2. Write out the answers in detail. Describe who you'd be, what you'd do, and how you'd feel once you've gotten that thing (be it romance, a job, a higher bank balance, a new house) that you want.

3. Now, start to be, do, and feel those things anyway — even before your wish has materialized! Why wait for bliss when you can have it now?

Be a loner.
That gives you time to wonder,
to search for the truth.
Have holy curiosity.
Make your life worth living.

Albert Einstein

BE SELFISH
In a Good Way

"Don't be selfish!" is an admonishment we've heard since pre-school, when we first learned to share our toys. Of course we must put aside our own needs sometimes so we can live and work with others. Selfless ideals like compassion, caring, and altruism are among the highest states of human love and behavior. Yet we can't express these ideals in a healthy manner if we don't first learn to nurture our deepest selves.

Tending to the self does not mean grabbing for more than our share. It simply means that we honor the voices and values of our heart and soul. Take 20 minutes or more each day to listen within through journaling, meditating, or walking in nature. In doing so, you will awaken your natural instincts to help, heal, care, and create.

EXERCISES *for Joy in Solitude*

The Art of Self-Care

Picture a child you love at the age of 4 or 5. Ask yourself what this child needs. A hand to hold? A hug? A meal cooked with love? Your attention? Time to play? Whatever it is, find a way to give yourself the same gift today.

The Royal Treatment

As you go about your morning routine of washing your face, dressing, and preparing your morning brew, treat yourself as you would treat visiting royalty. Lavish yourself with attention, care, kindness, and respect.

Smile for a Selfie

Dress in the clothes that make you feel like your best self and head to a spot where you feel truly at home. In this environment, pose for a self-portrait using your phone or the camera of your choice. Post this image on your computer's desktop or anyplace where it will remind you that you are a treasure of a being who deserves to be treated with exquisite care.

Random Acts

On strips of paper, write down sweet things you'd love someone to do for you for no special reason, such as buy you a treat or a trinket, give you a hand massage, offer you a compliment, or leave a love note under your pillow. Write down as many ideas as you can think of and place the strips of paper in a special envelope or container. At least once a week, pick one at random and perform that kindness for yourself.

As I walk solitary,
unattended,
Around me
I hear that éclat
of the world . . .

Walt Whitman, *Leaves of Grass*

Table for ONE

It seems every self-help book is saying the same thing: to truly love and be loved by another, you must first love yourself. But how do we fall in love with the one person we know will always be by our side? That is, how do we learn to love ourselves?

When we are ready to fall in love with someone else, we go on dates and get to know the other person. We exchange stories. We have dinner by candlelight and take long walks on the beach. Over time we learn to look for the best in that person. We come to love their soft belly and every freckle, birthmark, and blemish on their skin.

And so we must do the same things for ourselves. We listen to our own stories by writing them down in a journal or in letters we address to ourselves, or we tune in to our thoughts consciously through meditation. We can even make dates with ourselves to visit a favorite café, drive to the beach, or stop in to a bookstore and browse for an hour. The point is to treat yourself to a meaningful, playful, fun, delicious, or deeply satisfying experience to give yourself the attention and care you wish the perfect suitor would.

When you spend time with yourself in this way, you're not just stuck being alone; you're honored to spend time with your own fabulous self. So make time to woo yourself. Court yourself with flowers and treats. Enjoy the simple and delicious privilege of some quality time alone.

Going on solo dates, learning to be still and quiet on the meditation cushion and off, and making peace with your thoughts are all ways to learn to be at home in your own skin. Not only is this a deeply satisfying indulgence, it's the most important step in finding true and lasting happiness.

EXERCISES *for Joy in Solitude*

Soak It In

Add a few drops of lavender oil or lavender salts to a warm bath and step in. Lavender helps us relax and renew, and a warm tub is a great place for a mini-retreat away from the demands of the world.

Be Serenaded

Listen to love songs as if they were being sung just for you by a divine being (God, the universe, or your highest and best self).

Special Delivery

Buy your own flowers — don't wait for someone else to do it. Other people can add to your happiness, but the only one who can guarantee it is you.

Alone Time

Consider where, when, and how often you will make space for yourself, and block out times in your planner accordingly. Use the word *booked* to mark these appointments with yourself, so when someone requests time with you, you have an easy way to say your time is already spoken for. Or try saying, "To care for myself, I need to say no to that right now."

Little Luxuries

For a quick pick-me-up, soak two cotton makeup pads in warm water and add a few drops of rosewater. Lie down and place the pads, folded into half moons, on your eye pouches, and cover them with a warm folded washcloth or eye pillow. Rest for 10 to 20 minutes, enjoying the soothing scent and comforting sensation.

Make a Date

Browse the weekend listings in your local newspaper and make a list of fun things you'd enjoy doing, such as joining a guided hike, attending a chamber music concert, going to an art opening, or seeing an indie movie. Now choose a date to do one of them — by yourself.

At the Table

NURTURE YOURSELF: All too often we use food as a way to comfort ourselves — even when we're not hungry. Instead, look for simple ways to nurture yourself, such as taking a warm bath, reading quietly for an hour, or snuggling on the couch with a comfy blanket — rather than filling up on foods you don't really need.

BETTER BREAKFAST: After a breakfast of pancakes, sausage, and home fries, you'll likely feel sluggish. That's because high-carbohydrate foods increase the tryptophan (nature's sleeping medicine) released in your body. Also, heavy foods sap energy rather than restore it, because they are difficult for the body to digest. Instead, try a fruit salad with yogurt or a scrambled egg. You'll feel lighter and more focused as you begin your day.

LOVING SPOONFUL: Make it a habit to reflect on your intentions for the day at the breakfast table, and affirm them to yourself. These heart-centered goals might include a desire to be more loving and kind, to show your appreciation, or to choose trust rather than worry.

SET THE TABLE, SET YOUR MOOD: Make it a practice this week to set the table for each meal, whether you'll be dining alone or with others. Mindfully preparing the table helps you slow down and look forward to the pleasures of the meal to come.

YOU ARE THE RICE: In some Asian cultures, the everyday act of rinsing the rice before cooking it is treated with reverence. The love that is transferred to the food in this manner is considered an essential ingredient for the meal. You can apply this idea to how you approach the food you are cooking — or to the way you approach your own body. The next time you wash your hands, treat your skin with the same sacred attention that some devote to washing the rice.

Sitting quietly
doing nothing
spring comes
and the grass grows
by itself.

Matsuo Bashō

SIT DOWN
with Yourself

If you have a hard time keeping a positive attitude, don't add self-blame to the list of gloomy thoughts that plague you. Humans are hardwired to focus on negative emotions such as fear and anxiety. When life was a matter of moment-to-moment survival, this helped our ancient ancestors avoid predators and survive to see another sunrise. But these behaviors no longer serve us, and negative thinking just leads to despair and hopelessness.

But combating negative thinking is no easy feat. Thoughts pass through our mind all day, with or without our permission. At best, we can control where we put our attention and for how long. It's worth the effort, however, as your thoughts can make you feel anxious, fearful, or dejected. Sometimes your thoughts will make you feel happy, too. But unless you learn to be aware and direct your attention, chances are your thoughts will bring you down more often than they'll inspire and uplift you.

Ancient practices such as meditation, contemplation, and prayer can help us become aware of our thoughts and choose thoughts consciously. These practices have also been proven to have dramatic effects on mental health. Regular mindfulness meditation for 20 minutes a day has been shown to have an equal or better chance of lifting moods than antidepressant medication.

EXERCISES *for Joy in Solitude*

Meditation Motivation

Magazine articles, blogs, and health reports are filled with facts like this one: the brain areas associated with stress become less active when you meditate, while those associated with joy, peace, and compassion become energized. Collect more facts like this about the benefits of meditation, and use them to motivate you to sit in silence for 12 minutes or more each day.

Morning Brew

Having trouble figuring out where you can fit in a few minutes to meditate? Try sitting at the kitchen table and focusing on your breath while your coffee is brewing, while your phone or computer is powering on, or while you're waiting for your children to change into their pajamas before it's time to read them their bedtime story.

Listen to Yourself

We complain that others don't listen to us, but how well do we really listen to ourselves? You can consciously listen to yourself by tuning in to your thoughts through meditation, journaling, and checking in with internal chatter throughout the day.

Mind Games

Set the timer on your watch or phone, and see if you can stop your thoughts for a full minute. It's harder than you think. Try again. When you master one minute, try it for two. Can you get all the way to three? Go ahead, keep score . . . just remember, it's not whether you win or lose that matters; it's how joyfully you can play this game that counts.

Time to Let Go

Set an alert on your phone to chime at random intervals. When it does, notice what you'd been thinking. If your mind was wandering into negative territory, such as rehashing old wounds or looking for reasons to be sad, rein it in. Inhale deeply, and let go of negative thoughts as you exhale.

seven

Joy with Others

God gave us memory
so that we might have
roses in December.

J. M. Barrie

LOVE *One Another*

Sometimes it seems every song and every movie, every book and every story, is about love. But with so much evidence of love in the air, why does it sometimes seem so difficult to define, let alone find? Love is a verb. It is an action word. The power to create and access love is in your hands, heart, and mind. We don't need to be able to define what love is in order to feel it flow through our lives, nor do we need a definition to discover divine loving energy in our interactions with the people in our lives.

EXERCISES *for Joy with Others*

As If Your Heart Has Ears

When listening to a family member speak, shift your attention from your head to your heart, and see how the quality of your listening — and your interaction — changes.

Love Notes

Make a list of all the people in your life that you love. Now choose one and write a love letter recounting something she said or did recently that you appreciate, or describe the three qualities you love most about this person.

Sweet Somethings

Do something special — and unexpected — for someone today. Write a postcard to a faraway friend, or to one who lives around the corner. Do the dishes a coworker left in the lunchroom sink. Take a friend to tea, or pick up a pizza for a family member who's had a rough day.

Pay (Loving) Attention

Attention is the most loving gift of all. Today, give someone yours. Listen without planning what you will say in response. Show her with your body posture and by making eye contact that you are taking in what she has to say. Ask what you can do to offer support or lend a helping hand.

Let It Go

Don't wait for the person who wronged you to ask for it; grant forgiveness to someone today. Forget for a moment who is wrong or right — who owes whom a phone call, text, or message. Take a moment to reflect on what you loved about this person or relationship to begin with, and make the first move. Do it for your own happiness, and for your own heart's sake.

The Webs We Weave

Starting with yourself and working outward, identify all of the circles of support and community in your life:

1. **YOUR IMMEDIATE HOUSEHOLD** — self, family, roommates, and pets

2. **YOUR NEIGHBORHOOD** — your building or block, your community, your town

3. **YOUR VIRTUAL COMMUNITIES AND ASSOCIATIONS** — groups you engage with via social networks, online groups, or alumni associations, as well as any other foundations, organizations, associations, and networks of like-minded people you belong to

4. **THE HUMAN FAMILY** — people across all geographic borders and of all ages, races, and ethnicities

5. **ALL BEINGS, PLANTS, AND ANIMALS**

Take a few moments to contemplate your connection and kinship with each of the groups listed on the opposite page. Where are your bonds strongest? Where can your connections be revived or repaired? What surprises you about your list? Can you appreciate the extent of your web of connections and allow yourself to feel truly held and supported by these many bonds today?

Now consider one way you can strengthen your connections with the members of each of these groups. Is it time to make a phone call? Offer an apology? Invite a friend to dinner? Write a letter or sign a petition to show you care about a world issue? Choose one connection in need and take action on it this week.

A Seat at the TABLE

The kitchen table where your children once sat in booster seats and now sit poring over their high school homework; the café table on the sidewalk on a late summer afternoon where you meet a friend for tea and conversation; the holiday table you set with your best china and cloth napkins — and where your sister from across the country and your brother from across the state, and all of their children, and the family from next door, will gather at Thanksgiving; the long rectangular table in the boardroom where you meet with colleagues to create new visions for your company: each of these tables represents another link in the chain of connection that joins us to the people and communities that enrich our lives.

At these tables we gather to talk, laugh, argue, create, cry, listen, and grow. They are the tables where we share food or set out our papers and plans. These are the places where we are nourished in body and soul; they are where meaning and memories are born.

Whether you gather at a physical table or connect online, in dance halls, classrooms, community rooms, or church basements, notice the various communities you belong to. The quality of your circles of connection has a lot to do with how you experience meaning and joy in your life. So become conscious of what you bring to the table, who meets you there, and whether and how you feel fed when you arrive.

EXERCISES *for Joy with Others*

Go-To List

Make a list of the three to five most supportive people in your life, and post it where you'll see it when you need it. You might write these names on a slip of paper and tuck it between the pages in your journal or in your billfold. Or you might use this list to create a special contact folder in your cell phone. Call someone on this list when you need a listening ear or a comforting voice.

Muscle Groups

Exercise isn't a chore if you do it with someone you care about. Invite a neighbor to take a brisk walk with you, play catch with your dog, or go dancing with your spouse.

Post It

Scroll through your recent status updates, and notice whether your posts are in line with the values you most want to uphold. Technology gives us an unprecedented opportunity to share meaning, love, and caring with others. But we can also mindlessly add to the noise of the Internet, creating more distraction at best — or spreading harmful speech at worst.

Link In

Studies show that it is how we use social media that determines whether it enriches our lives or drains our energy. Make the time you spend with your virtual social circles more meaningful by using social networks to stay in touch with people you'd like to spend time with face to face, setting intentions before you log on, and logging off when you notice your online activity is devolving into lurking, bragging, judging, or comparing.

Only connect!

E. M. Forster, *Howard's End*

Regain Balance

We love our families, but closeness can be complicated. To regain equanimity when you've been thrown off balance, practice Tree Pose to help you regain your footing. In addition to the physical benefits, Tree Pose helps improve concentration, memory, and focus.

1. Stand with your arms at your sides and your feet close together but not touching.

2. Gradually shift your weight to your left foot and lift your right foot as high as you comfortably can.

3. Place your right foot on your left leg, using your hand to guide it. Let the foot rest against your ankle, just below the knee (never on the knee), or on your thigh.

4. Gently gaze at a point on the wall in front of you to help stay focused and balanced.

5. Place your hands in prayer position in front of your chest, or raise them in the air above your head. You can also hold onto the wall for support.

6. Feel your standing foot root into the earth and your arms extend like branches into the air.

7. Hold the pose for several breaths, and then repeat it on the other side.

Brimming with JOY

Order a cup of sake (fermented rice wine) in Japan, and you might find that your server pours until the wine splashes over the edges of the cup and into the saucer. This isn't a lapse on the server's part; it's a symbolic gesture indicating abundance and generosity.

Another Japanese custom is to pass the saucer and share with your companions the sake that spilled over, to symbolically share your joys. This is a beautiful tradition that reminds us to increase the sweetness of life by giving some away. We can also use this sentiment as a reminder to affirm the flow of abundant goodness in our lives.

Consider how you can share your joys with others, whether it's by adopting the Japanese ceremony of sharing the overflow of sweet wine, or by sharing smiles, blessings, and kind words. That's something we can all raise a glass to, and say *"kanpai!"* (kahn-pie) — Japanese for *Cheers*!

My cup runneth over.

Psalm 23:5

EXERCISES *for Joy with Others*

Gesundheit

Good moods spread like the flu. So don't hide your joy. Let someone know how happy you feel today, and wish the same for him. Let your joy go viral.

A Round of Joy

Studies show that people who perform five acts of kindness per week for 6 weeks enjoy an increased level of happiness. Helping others improves our self-esteem and our sense of purpose — and thus makes us smile inside and out.

Fill the Bowl

Imagine your smile is a bowl you can fill with happy thoughts and memories. Then go ahead and picture each drop of joy raining down and filling your grin. You might have to smile a little bit bigger just to hold it all.

Smile!

Back in the seventies they were ubiquitous: yellow smiley faces decorating everything from jewelry to T-shirts to trash cans. Now they're back in the form of emoticons and pulsing emoji. If any symbol has earned its right to flood our consciousness, it's the smiley face. Smiles are contagious. When we smile we get happier, and when we smile at others we spread the joy. Try this smiling meditation:

1. Smile with your lips as you enjoy one to three slow, conscious breaths.

2. Smile with the whole inside of the mouth as you enjoy one to three slow, conscious breaths.

3. Feel a smile spread across your throat as you enjoy one to three slow, conscious breaths.

4. Feel a smile spread across your forehead as you enjoy one to three slow, conscious breaths.

Repeat as often as you like, and best of all, bring your smile with you wherever you go today.

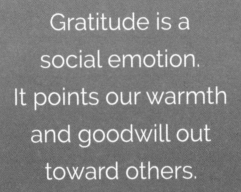

Gratitude is a
social emotion.
It points our warmth
and goodwill out
toward others.

Joanna Macy and Chris Johnstone,
Active Hope

THANK-YOU *Notes*

Growing up we had to be cajoled into saying please and thank you. "What do you say?" our mothers had to beseech us each time we were complimented or given a lollipop. We had to be told to write thank-you notes when we received a gift. But now we know that saying thank you is more than just good manners. Quite simply, people who express gratitude are happier. Saying thank you burns away bad moods and helps keep us humble; it's a generous attitude that softens the heart. That's a lot of power behind two simple syllables.

Knowing that gratitude is the fast track to feeling good, why not encourage yourself to say thank you out loud to others — or silently to yourself, God, or to the universe — any time you feel appreciative?

EXERCISES *for Joy with Others*

Apple for the Teacher

When you accomplish something small or large, think with appreciation of all the teachers (official and unofficial) who enabled you to gain the skills and qualities that contributed to your success. Send one of them a thank-you note.

Gratitude Adjustment

When you have an unproductive negative thought, stop and think of three things you are truly grateful for. Start small, with the things you tend to overlook. When's the last time you appreciated having toes? Felt grateful for the custodian in the office building where you work? Thanked the bees for pollinating those flowers you enjoy gazing at outside your window?

Everyday Miracles

Next time you feel appreciative of something, think of all the people who made it possible. Eating a slice of toast? Think about what went into growing the wheat, harvesting it, baking it into bread, transporting the loaves, and stocking those loaves on the shelves in the store. Notice the everyday miracles that enrich your life.

Thanks, Mom

Start a family gratitude journal, in which each person notes something they are grateful for about that day. Look for the small things we tend to skip past, like a vibrant color, the taste of a favorite food, or the sound of a child's laughter. Designate a few minutes after dinner or before bed to read aloud the newest entries together.

Under ONE ROOF

Those bygone days of sitting in the family room arguing over which channel to watch on TV now seem quaint and lucky. These days, with multiple television sets in most American households — and with tablets, smartphones, and laptops — it's easy enough to spend time together with loved ones, but all too often each is interacting with his own device and engaged in a different activity. It is an irony of our age that in the midst of all of our hyperconnectivity, truly connecting with family and friends in meaningful ways is more challenging than ever. Old-school face time fosters deep relationships, connection, caring, support, and love. With a little effort and ingenuity we can reclaim our authentic relationships and use today's technology to augment, not replace, them.

EXERCISES *for Joy with Others*

Check Please

Make this playful pact with friends: the first one to check her phone during a dinner out pays the bill. This lighthearted incentive will quickly reduce the number of phone-related distractions and help bring you closer together.

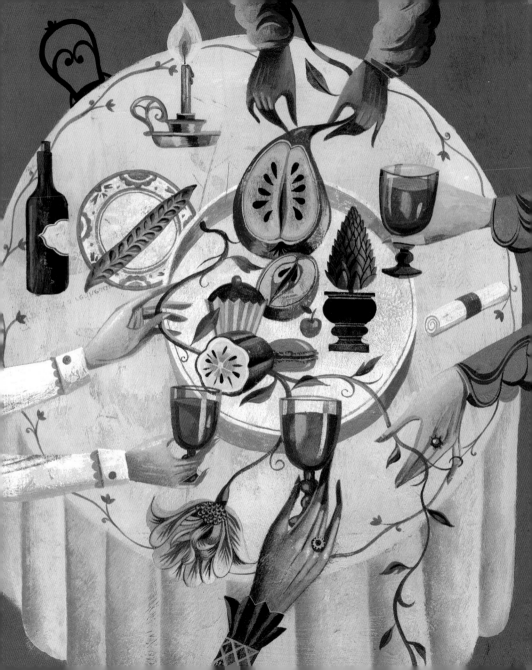

Happiness
[is] only real
when shared.

Jon Krakauer,
Into the Wild

Declare a Screen-Free Zone

Make mealtimes screen-free zones, or designate "unplugged" hours as times to be together playing card games, doing puzzles, talking, or doing projects together.

Reality Show

Instead of watching one more TV show where people parade their talents, designate an evening to create your own. Host a playful competition in your living room for the best performance of a dance number, song, or story, and let the fun begin. Bestow awards for funniest, corniest, most inspired, or most original performance so that everyone is recognized with humor and love.

Cellular Awareness

Become conscious of your cell phone use when you're in someone else's company. Turn off the ringer if possible, and always put the person you are with before the incoming call or text.

Virtual Buddy

If your ideal exercise partner lives far away, plan a time you will both hop on the treadmill or take a walk, each in your own location. Connect by cell phone and have a virtual exercise date.

The wide world
is all about you:
you can fence yourselves in,
but you cannot forever
fence it out.

J. R. R. Tolkien,
The Fellowship of the Ring

In the NEIGHBORHOOD

In the poem "Mending Wall," Robert Frost famously wrote, "Good fences make good neighbors." It is true that fences, both literal and metaphorical, help us set and maintain healthy boundaries. But as Frost also writes in his poem, it is important to consider what we are walling in and what we are keeping out when we build a barrier. Backyard fences can be places where neighbors take a break and talk to one another, or they can become cold markers of separation.

Interestingly, for many people tearing down fences brings more happiness than putting them up. In some neighborhoods around the country, people are removing fences and creating common spaces for neighborly picnics, play areas, and gardens. Making space for meaningful interactions with neighbors is one way people are breaking isolation and finding increased joy in their lives.

EXERCISES *for Joy with Others*

Keep It Local

Pair up with a neighbor to create seasonal, locally sourced potlucks for residents of your block or building. Make it a fun challenge to cook up recipes that use as many local ingredients as possible.

Sidewalk Talk

Simply stepping outside helps create and foster a sense of community: take your morning coffee out of the kitchen and sip it on the front stoop, walk your dog around the block rather than just letting her out in the yard, or forgo home delivery and instead walk to the store for your newspaper.

Know Thy Neighbor

Start a neighborhood email group where you can share information about relevant community issues, offer shared resources from lawn mowers to babysitting, and help one another locate lost pets. Get the conversations started online and keep them going on the sidewalk.

Third Space

The concept of a third place — a space that's neither home nor work — has become an important idea in community building. Find a place in your neighborhood, such as a café or park, and invite neighbors and friends to gather there for an hour after work and before dinner at a set time each week. You don't need an agenda — just a friendly space for conversation and connection.

If I can't dance,
it's not my revolution.

Emma Goldman

JOY *to the World*

These days, with environmental crises looming and political upheavals erupting around the globe, it's hard to let ourselves gaze too far beyond the scope of our daily concerns. Anxiety and hopelessness creep into our vision, and we can too easily choose to close our eyes to what's going on around us.

We may feel alone in our grief and confusion about the state of the world, but many people share our concerns. A culture of isolation, however, keeps us from realizing we are all connected, and the earth beneath our feet is our common lineage. By finding productive ways to express our concerns through journaling, art, conversation with loved ones, and joining community groups around issues we care about, we let our feelings flow. And then we feel strengthened to respond to the needs of our world with a heart full of compassion, caring, and appropriate action.

EXERCISES *for Joy with Others*

Altruism Is Selfish

It is a little-known fact that altruism — taking compassionate action on behalf of others — actually increases feelings of happiness. So for the world's sake, and for your own, devote some of your time and energy to doing something for the greater good.

Care and Connect

Does your heart ache when you hear about the effects of factory farming on animals? Do you get choked up when you hear about a natural disaster in a far-off country? Do you find yourself arguing for increased funding for education? Find a way to engage with others to address injustices in the world, and replace cynicism, frustration, or heartbreak with purpose, connection, and optimism.

Feel into Action

Take time to feel your grief and despair. Turning away only makes your mood worse, as you struggle to tamp down your feelings of helplessness. After you grieve, take action. Even a small, symbolic gesture, such as lighting a candle in honor of innocent people who've died in a far-off war, helps our loving hearts begin to heal.

From Guilt to Gratitude

Too often we do good out of guilt, but your good increases when, instead, you act out of gratitude and love for what you want to protect and nourish.

Renewable Resources

Next time you turn off a light to save electricity, consider your own personal energy needs, as well. Are you respecting your inner resources and taking time to replenish your stores of hope and love?

Give a Little

Research has shown that 20 minutes a day of loving-kindness (metta) meditation can be as effective as medication in boosting moods. There are many forms of metta meditation and instructions are available in various books on meditation or on the Internet. Here are simple instructions to get you started.

1. Sit quietly, and breathe into your heart.

2. Think about something you love about yourself, and feel your heart fill with appreciation.

3. Direct three to five simple heartfelt wishes to yourself, such as, "May I be happy, may I be loved, and may I live in peace." Repeat these wishes several times, coordinating the phrases with your breath.

4. Now think of someone you love unconditionally, such as a family member or child, and do the same for her.

5. Repeat this exercise of filling your heart with love and extending gratitude to someone in each of your circles. Continue to move outward to a friend, then an acquaintance, a stranger, someone with whom you have a difficult relationship, and finally all people and all beings.

Try doing this meditation for 20 minutes or more each day. Don't be discouraged if this feels difficult at first. Extending loving-kindness to all people without exception isn't easy. Be gentle with yourself, and if you get stuck, simply return to directing loving-kindness to yourself or someone you love unconditionally. Over time it will become easier — and deeply pleasurable.

eight

Joyful Celebration

Every sunset
is a pilgrimage
to the sunrise.

Every time
you miss the sunset,
you miss the beautiful
beginning of the
holy journey!

Mehmet Murat ildan

SUNRISE, SUNSET

Starting at about two hours before sunset, the sidewalks of Key West, Florida, begin to fill with tourists and locals, all walking toward Mallory Square. There the pier is bustling with clowns, mimes, psychics, jugglers, local musicians, and people lined up at food stands. But the real attraction is hovering just above the horizon. As the sun sinks into the Gulf of Mexico, crowds line up four deep and shoulder to shoulder at the water's edge to watch wide-eyed as the sky blazes orange and pink — a dazzling display of natural light that is different every night. It's free of charge, and for all its extraordinary beauty, it's just as ordinary as a cloud or a blade of grass. There is something primal within us that draws us toward this ritual of communal appreciation for nature's gifts.

Our daily routines rarely leave time for us to sit and appreciate a sunset, let alone a sunrise. We are by and large cut off from nature's cycles. Most days we don't know what crops are ripening in our region, let alone what phase the moon is in. Yet noticing and honoring the cycles of nature — the rising and setting sun and moon, the turning of the stars and the seasons — can bring us into harmony with the world we inhabit, and doing so gives us an excuse to celebrate the extraordinary ordinary movements of our world.

EXERCISES *for Joyful Celebration*

Moon Gazing

It's a dark shadow in the night sky when it's new, a silvery and slivery smile waxing night by night, and a glowing globe that startles us as we drive home in the early dusk of an October evening when it's full. The moon that guides the tides and influences our sleep once ruled the calendar and marked holy days, such as feast and fast days, but in our busy lives we rarely take a moment to admire it. For one month, make it a practice to gaze nightly into the sky, note the moon's phase, and affirm your connection to nature and its cycles.

Wish Upon a Star

The new moon is said to be a powerful time to make wishes, and it's also the time when stars shine brightest. So go ahead, wish upon a star when the moon is new — and don't forget to glow a little brighter.

Phase of Life

Choose a way you'd like to nurture your soul, whether it be to go dancing, listen to music, attend a poetry reading, or make a painting — and put it on the calendar at a new moon, a full moon, a solstice, or an equinox. Let this be your personal holiday of renewal.

All of this like

some ancient anointing.

So be it.

Evoke the forms.

Where you've nothing else

construct ceremonies

out of the air and breathe

upon them.

Cormac McCarthy, *The Road*

Ceremonial
HAPPINESS

Each morning you pour your cereal into the painted bowl your daughter made you for a long-ago birthday and tune the radio to the same station. When you return home from work you sit in the same chair with your feet on the ottoman and do a crossword puzzle before you begin to prepare dinner. At night, you sit up in bed and read for 10 minutes, say the same prayer you've repeated since childhood, and go to sleep. We each have small rituals that we perform each day, and science confirms what we already suspect — they make us happy.

A ritual need not entail candlelight and prayers or a complex ceremony to have meaning. But repeated actions associated with certain activities, such as eating or going to bed, can make us more mindful and therefore increase the pleasures we experience.

EXERCISES *for Joyful Celebration*

Transition Time

Choose a time of day when you feel a bit of friction, such as transitioning from work to home or getting into bed at a reasonable hour. Institute or recharge an existing ritual to help make a tricky transition more pleasurable.

Goodbye and Hello

Create a ritual with family or friends to let go of things that are holding you back (fears, old resentments, grudges, worn out or harmful beliefs) and invite qualities such as love, compassion, and faith into your life. A ritual can be as simple as lighting a candle, taking turns speaking from the heart, planting a seed symbolizing your hopes, or tossing twigs that represent things you want to let go of into a nearby stream.

How You Eat an Oreo

Studies show that a simple ritual before eating makes the food taste better. Anything from mindfully unwrapping a candy bar to saying a prayer of thanks can work magic. Create your own food-related ritual to help you savor the flavors even more.

The soul
becomes dyed
with the color
of its thoughts.

Marcus Aurelius

Celebrate COLOR

Color is another extraordinary gift of ordinary life. The rainbow hues that surround us each day are a joy to experience. Color can be a source of inspiration as well as an invitation to admire and delight in the artistic palette of the natural world and our surroundings. Colors also affect our psychological state of being. According to the study of chakras, or internal energy centers, each color of the rainbow is said to have particular energetic and healing properties. Becoming conscious of color can help you move out of depressing grays and into the Technicolor splendor of your life.

EXERCISES *for Joyful Celebration*

Orange Juice

The second chakra, located at the navel center, is an energy center in the body associated with sensual pleasure, happiness, and creativity. This chakra is attuned to the color orange. So when you need a boost, imagine a ball of sunset-orange light emanating from the space just behind your belly button. Take several long, slow breaths as you imagine the sunset-orange glow growing stronger — and let the joyful feelings surge.

Color Is the New Black

If you are prone to dressing in grays and blacks, add a dash of color to your outfit. Put on a colorful shirt or tie, or accessorize with a pair of purple earrings or a colorful band around your hat.

Green Living

Nature paints lavishly with the color green — a color that is said to be soothing and healing to our soul. Look outside a window today, and focus on the green leaves of a tree or a green stretch of lawn. Or add potted plants to your indoor environment. Let your gaze go green from time to time, and enjoy the relaxing and rejuvenating effects.

Orange You Glad

Draw the energy of the second chakra to you all day long by wearing an orange shirt or camisole, or drape yourself with an orange scarf. Each time you see the color orange, stop and bring your attention to the qualities of the second chakra: pleasure, creativity, and joy.

God gave us the gift of life;
it is up to us to give ourselves
the gift of living well.

Voltaire

GIVE & RECEIVE

It seems that the Halloween pumpkins have barely been discarded before Christmas carols are playing in the stores. Complaints about the holidays becoming too commercial are rampant, and sometimes we're so busy hunting for bargains online or racing from store to store to find the perfect present that we forget what exactly we're celebrating, anyway.

Gift giving doesn't have to be a purely material pursuit; it is in essence a spiritual act in which the present you wrap is a tangible symbol of the love and appreciation you have for the recipient. When approached this way, gift-giving holidays become something you truly look forward to as an opportunity to feel and spread joy.

EXERCISES *for Joyful Celebration*

Celebrate the Small Stuff

Hallmark is famous for creating holidays to celebrate everything from secretaries to sisters to friendship to poetry. It's easy to scoff at the commercialism behind declaring so many holidays, but why not find something to celebrate every day? Go ahead, create your own holiday this week. Honor a family member, a delicious food, or even the start of the latest season of your favorite television show.

It's in the Cards

Make a greeting card rather than buy one, or personalize a store-bought card with stickers or collaged pictures. Adding a little creativity goes a long way in expressing your unique flavor of love.

Wrap It in Love

Make gift-wrapping an opportunity for calm contemplation. As you choose the paper, size it, fold it, and tie on a ribbon, hold an image of the recipient in your mind. Connect with the joy of giving your love and attention to that person as you prepare his gift.

Take the Compliment

When someone gives you the gift of praise, positive feedback, or kind words, enjoy the moment. Inhale slowly and deeply as you consciously receive the loving words, then exhale with a smile and a sincere "Thank you." Accepting, rather than deflecting, compliments makes us feel good and builds self-esteem.

Something for Everyone

Give a gift to everyone you meet today. Don't worry; it won't break the bank. You can give a smile, a compliment, a few moments of your complete attention, eye contact, a warm handshake, or a heartfelt hug.

Lose something
every day.
Accept the fluster
of lost door keys,
the hour badly spent.
The art of losing
isn't hard to master.

Elizabeth Bishop, *"One Art"*

MOURNING
Our Losses

Day to day, we try so hard to hold on to what we have. But reminders of what is lost surround us: makeshift memorials to loved ones who've passed appear in the form of bouquets and wooden crosses arranged to create roadside shrines that honor someone who died in a crash. A ghostly white bicycle chained to a city signpost pays tribute to a cyclist who was run down. A stone cairn beside a riverbed marks an unnamed mourner's grief. And a flag flown at half-mast honors a government official who has died.

Grief must be fully felt, acknowledged, and released if we are to heal and move forward in our lives. And it's not only when we lose a loved one that we need to find an appropriate way to mourn. We face losses large and small throughout our lives. In addition to losing people and pets we've loved, we also lose relationships, jobs, and houses. We might even mourn parts of ourselves that we must let go as we move from one phase of life to the next. Even a positive change, such as getting a new job, means we need to let go of the old.

Unless we grieve what we've lost, we can't fully experience what we have. But there is no shortcut in this journey. We have to feel the full range of emotions that accompany goodbyes in order to heal and grow and to once more welcome the return of happiness and joy.

EXERCISES *for Joyful Celebration*

Heartfelt Endings

If only we could let go as easily as a snake rubs against a rock and sheds its old skin, or as effortlessly as a maple tree drops its leaves in autumn. But accepting loss is not easy. The first step is to notice how natural it is to let go: nighttime ends to make room for day, we say goodbye to a friend after sharing a pot of tea and move on, we complete tasks at the office and head home. Today, notice each commonplace ending and how you feel as you let go of one thing and move on to the next.

Saying Goodbye

Make a list of losses you've experienced. Ask yourself if you've truly grieved and said goodbye, or if you're still holding on. Create a simple and heartfelt ceremony to honor the beauty of the person or situation that has passed, feel the sorrow, and allow yourself the gift of letting go. Write a goodbye letter, plant a tree, or light a candle to honor your process of moving forward and celebrating new growth.

Unending Love

Each life ends, but love is eternal. Create an album or scrapbook to honor someone that you've lost, and affirm that your heart is richer for the memories you've shared.

I celebrate myself,
and sing myself...

Walt Whitman,
"Song of Myself"

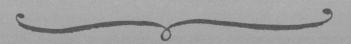

YAY YOU!

A child takes her first step, and we burst into spontaneous applause and hugs. We then mark the day in her baby book with pictures and words of glowing praise. It's not a holiday marked on any calendar, but in the record of our family's life, it's a red-letter day for sure. As adults, however, we seldom mark our milestones, aside from weddings and birthdays. There are many small but still significant events along the way that get lost in the shuffle. We get a promotion at work, or let go of an old relationship; we run our first mile, or complete a month of sticking to a healthy eating plan — but where are the balloons? Do we even share the news with our friends? What do we do to mark the moment?

Celebrating ourselves is more than mere self-indulgence; it's self-care. In fact, we're hardwired for rewards, and the more we give ourselves positive feedback, the better we feel. Neuroscience shows us that when we celebrate a success, our brain delivers a pleasurable dose of dopamine. Not only does this make us feel happier, it also makes it more likely that we'll succeed again, as the neural pathways of success have been strengthened. So celebrating personal accomplishments can help make way for more happiness and more success.

Consciously choose which accomplishments and meaningful milestones — whether large or small — you will mark and how you want to celebrate. Any excuse for a party, right?

EXERCISES *for Joyful Celebration*

Stand Up for Joy

Stand tall and raise your arms overhead in a *V*. Hold this pose for 1 or 2 minutes, or for as long as is comfortable. This posture decreases levels of cortisol (a stress hormone) and increases testosterone, making you feel relaxed and happy.

Birthday Present

On your special day, look for one intangible gift for each year of your age. On your 30th birthday find 30 gifts, at 47 find 47, and so on. Receive each small beauty or magical moment on that day as a special gift given to you from the world: the fresh smell in the air just before it begins to snow, the giddy birthday song your daughter sings to you, the barking of the sea lion you glimpsed at the zoo. Each year, as the number of gifts on your list increases and you strengthen the habit of looking for presents in the present moment all year long, the task becomes easier.

Certificates of Achievement

At the end of each day, write down three things that went well. Perhaps you kept calm during a stressful conversation, you made time to eat a healthy breakfast despite your packed agenda, and you had a productive day at work. Now note why you were successful in these areas. Do this for a week or more, and you will be rewarded with increased feelings of joy and satisfaction for months to come.

Cheers to You

Make it a tradition to gather with family or friends on a set night each week to appreciate one another's accomplishments. Go around the table, and each name a success that you experienced that week. Clink your glasses and toast one another's progress.

epilogue

The Cycle of Joy

It ain't over
'til it's over.

Yogi Berra

NO END *to Joy*

The instructions on a shampoo bottle offer an excellent model for living an intentional life: lather, rinse, repeat. We actively cleanse our minds of negative thinking and suds up with ebullient new ways of seeing the world. We breathe into our new happiness, and then we find ourselves once again in a funk of despair. And so . . . we begin again.

Living a joyful life is a cycle of active effort to create or reinvigorate healthy habits of thinking and being, reaching a new level of contentment and engagement — and repeating the process as often as necessary.

We can choose to wake up and delight in ordinary miracles such as the sight of blades of grass poking through spring soil, a flock of red-winged blackbirds swirling into flight, or rain curtaining a lake on a summer day. Every moment is an invitation to start over and to see the world anew.

Likewise, reaching the end of this book is an invitation to begin again and renew your passion for living more fully. Like the meditator sitting on a cushion who continually comes back to her breath each time her mind wanders, you, too, will bring yourself back to your intention to live your best life. You will return, time and again, to the practice of reaching for the good that lies beneath the stress and the frustration, the regret, the anxiety, the shoulds, and the have-tos.

Creating increased joy and meaning is a lifestyle. With time it will come to feel natural to choose love over fear, or to gently coax your mind away from an old, worn-out negative belief that no longer serves you and toward a fresh perspective on the situation at hand.

So when you close the covers of this book, don't just tuck it back on the shelf and forget about it. Open it again each time you need a gentle nudge or a friendly chuck on the shoulder reminding you to be your best self. Reach for it when you can use a whispered enticement to let go of your negative thinking and wake up to the wonder of this moment.

EXERCISES *for the Joy of It*

Progress, Not Perfection

Look back to when you first picked up this book and notice any changes in attitude or behavior you've adopted since then. Thinking about this, raise your right arm overhead, bend it at the elbow so your fingertips reach toward the floor behind you, and give yourself a well-deserved pat on the back for your progress. Simply creating the intention to live better is reason enough for reward.

Turning the Page

When you find yourself turning the final pages in this book, it is a good time to renew your commitment to joy. Drawing from the tips you've found here, choose three easy ones that you'll commit to integrating into your life for the next month. Write them down in your planner, on your to-do lists, or in your journal to help yourself remember.

Consciousness Raising

Back in the '70s, consciousness-raising groups were popular for women wanting to reclaim their voices and their personal and political power. Today, create a Joy-Raising Group. Invite several friends to join you, and meet weekly or monthly in person or by conference call to discuss ways you are each using the exercises in this book. Gently hold each other accountable with a check-in during which you share successes, intentions, and strategies for support as you continue to move toward your deepest joy.

A Backward Glance

A productive way to evaluate any experience is to address the "Three Whats": What Happened? So What? and What Now?

Thinking back over the days, weeks, or months since you first started practicing the suggestions in these pages, reflect in your journal on these questions.

1. **WHAT HAPPENED?** Briefly describe your journey into joy. Since you first picked up this book, what tips did you try, and what were the results? What worked best for you? What do you still want to try?

2. **SO WHAT?** Ask yourself why this quest for increased feelings of contentment and gladness matters. What has been the significance for you of embarking on a more joyful and meaningful life? Why is it important to stick with your intentions to live fully in each moment?

3. **WHAT NOW?** You've reached a milestone by completing this book. How will you celebrate this success? What would you like to do now to continue your commitment to waking up to joy? What ideas and practices from this book will you take with you into the future?

NOT

The End

joy jottings

The last time I felt really happy was:

_____

_____

_____

My earliest memory of feeling joyful is:

_____

_____

_____

_____

A color that makes me happy is:

_____

My favorite time of day is:

_____

_____

Three people who I feel happiest with are:

When I'm sad, the sound of this person's voice can cheer me up:

A scent that brings a smile to my face is:

It might sound crazy, but I really enjoy:

joy drawings

PICTURING JOY

Get out your crayons or colored pencils and scribble or sketch something that makes you happy.

JOY-QUEST

Draw a map of your favorite place, real or imaginary.

Other Storey Books You Will Enjoy

Clear the Clutter, Find Happiness *by Donna Smallin*
Finally, a way to get rid of the clutter — and keep it away — without making the process a full-time job! These motivating tips and tricks will help you clean, organize, and relax in your daily life. Put your mind and home at ease!
288 pages. Paper. ISBN 978-1-61212-351-6.

The Curious Nature Guide *by Clare Walker Leslie*
Step outside and reinvigorate your senses with help from Clare Walker Leslie's inviting guide to expanding your creativity. Use prompts, facts, beautiful photography, and inspiring artwork to navigate through nature and see the world anew.
144 pages. Paper with flaps. ISBN 978-1-61212-509-1.

Live More, Want Less *by Mary Carlomagno*
With 52 ways to find order in your life, simplicity expert Mary Carlomagno presents a theme for every week, along with daily practice suggestions for stripping away the nonessentials that keep you from living a full, meaningful life.
192 pages. Paper. ISBN 978-1-60342-558-2.

Wabi Sabi *by Diane Durston*
This beautiful little book celebrates nature's simplicity and the beauty of imperfection with photographs, inspirational quotes, and reflections on the classic Japanese approach to bringing greater mindfulness to daily life.
384 pages. Paper. ISBN 978-1-58017-628-6.

These and other books from Storey Publishing are available
wherever quality books are sold or by calling 1-800-441-5700.
Visit us at *www.storey.com* or sign up for our newsletter
at *www.storey.com/signup.*